# STARFINDER

**Development Leads** • Jason Keeley and Chris S. Sims

**Authors** • Chris S. Sims, with Stephen Glicker, Jason Keeley, Epidiah Ravachol, Owen K.C. Stephens, and James L. Sutter

**Cover Artist** • Ignacio Bazán Lazcano

**Interior Artists** • Dave Melvin, Mark Molnar, and Ainur Salimova

**Page Border Design** • Graey Erb

**Cartographer** • Damien Mammoliti

**Creative Directors** • James Jacobs, Robert G. McCreary, and Sarah E. Robinson

**Director of Game Design** • Jason Bulmahn

**Managing Developers** • Adam Daigle and Amanda Hamon Kunz

**Organized Play Lead Developer** • John Compton

**Developers** • Eleanor Ferron, Jason Keeley, Luis Loza, Ron Lundeen, Joe Pasini, Michael Sayre, Chris S. Sims, and Linda Zayas-Palmer

**Starfinder Design Lead** • Owen K.C. Stephens

**Starfinder Society Developer** • Thurston Hillman

**Senior Designer** • Stephen Radney-MacFarland

**Designers** • Logan Bonner and Mark Seifter

**Managing Editor** • Judy Bauer

**Senior Editor** • Christopher Carey

**Editors** • James Case, Leo Glass, Lyz Liddell, Adrian Ng, Lacy Pellazar, and Jason Tondro

**Art Director** • Sonja Morris

**Senior Graphic Designers** • Emily Crowell and Adam Vick

**Franchise Manager** • Mark Moreland

**Project Manager** • Gabriel Waluconis

**Publisher** • Erik Mona

**Paizo CEO** • Lisa Stevens

**Chief Operations Officer** • Jeffrey Alvarez

**Chief Financial Officer** • John Parrish

**Chief Technical Officer** • Vic Wertz

**Director of Sales** • Pierce Watters

**Sales Associate** • Cosmo Eisele

**Vice President of Marketing & Licensing** • Jim Butler

**Marketing Manager** • Dan Tharp

**Licensing Manager** • Glenn Elliott

**Public Relations Manager** • Aaron Shanks

**Organized Play Manager** • Tonya Woldridge

**Human Resources Generalist** • Megan Gilchrist

**Accountant** • Christopher Caldwell

**Data Entry Clerk** • B. Scott Keim

**Web Production Manager** • Chris Lambertz

**Senior Software Developer** • Gary Teter

**Webstore Coordinator** • Rick Kunz

**Customer Service Team** • Sharaya Copas, Katina Davis, Virginia Jordan, Sara Marie, Samantha Phelan, and Diego Valdez

**Warehouse Team** • Laura Wilkes Carey, Will Chase, Mika Hawkins, Heather Payne, Jeff Strand, and Kevin Underwood

**Website Team** • Brian Bauman, Robert Brandenburg, Whitney Chatterjee, Erik Keith, and Andrew White

## ON THE COVER

Something's not quite right with brutaris champion Yazeloya Golkami in this chilling cover by artist Ignacio Bazán Lazcano.

## CONTENT WARNING

The Signal of Screams Adventure Path contains typical Starfinder action and adventure, but be warned that it also presents scenarios in which horrifying things happen to the PCs and the NPCs around them. The events presented in this Adventure Path fall into the realm of body horror and psychological horror, which can include disfigurement, mutation, parasitism and disease, self-mutilation, injury, and the aftermath of such unpleasantness. Before you begin, understand that player consent (including that of the GM) is the most important thing to consider. GMs should talk with their players about the horror elements included and obtain everyone's consent to the inclusion of these topics. It's also a good idea to include a method for players to indicate whether the game's content has gone too far during play. More instruction about running horror campaigns responsibly and ensuring that all players have fun is included in the article "Horror Campaigns" on page 46.

This book refers to several other Starfinder products using the following abbreviations, yet these additional supplements are not required to make use of this book. Readers interested in references to Starfinder hardcovers can find the complete rules of these books available online for free at **sfrd.info**.

| | | | |
|---|---|---|---|
| *Armory* | AR | *Pact Worlds* | PW |

**Paizo Inc.**
7120 185th Ave NE, Ste 120
Redmond, WA 98052-0577
**paizo.com**

# WE HAVE SUCH SIGHTS TO SHOW YOU

When the funding for her research into the nature and cause of pain started to run out, the brilliant scientist Dr. Lestana Gragant was approached by Eclipse Innovations, a corporation that proposed Dr. Gragant shift the focus of her research to military applications. She was relocated to a secret facility on an asteroid in the Diaspora and put under constant pressure to produce results.

As time passed, Dr. Gragant grew desperate, and one fateful day, she enacted a mostly theoretical technomagical procedure on herself. It resulted in a mystical implosion that killed all of Dr. Gragant's subjects and assistants, drew large portions of the facility into the Shadow Plane, and transformed the doctor into a half-velstrac fiend the likes of which the universe had never seen. Eclipse Innovations covered up the evidence of the accident as best they could and shelved Dr. Gragant's research.

Forever changed, Dr. Gragant spent the next 13 years on the Shadow Plane, where she lost any lingering compassion for others. She began to see pain and suffering as gifts she could bring to the Material Plane, and she got the chance to do so when the asteroid where her research facility had been located was turned into a luxury resort named New Elysium. She reached out to twist the mind of Kaeon Rhyse, an Eclipse Innovations executive who was visiting the resort. With Kaeon's help, she soon had most of Eclipse's employees under her control. She then had her minions craft a way to transmit her corrupting influence through a program on a comm unit, which Eclipse then sold to New Elysium as a virtual concierge. The resort is about to hold a gala celebrating this technology, and the PCs are invited!

## THE DIASPORA STRAIN
**By Chris S. Sims**
*Starfinder Adventure Path* #10, Levels 7–8

A vacation to New Elysium—a luxury resort located on an asteroid in the Diaspora—begins to go horribly wrong as the facilities malfunction and the guests and staff turn violent. The heroes must protect themselves and aid those who have resisted the corrupting influence, including a wealthy android tech entrepreneur who might have information about the cause of this malady. Once rescued from the old mining tunnels beneath the resort, the android reveals the true source of the problem: the virtual concierge installed in everyone's

## CAMPAIGN OUTLINE
### Spoiler Alert!
On this page you'll find the background and outline for the Signal of Screams Adventure Path. If you intend to play in this campaign, be warned! This page spoils the plot for the upcoming adventures as thoroughly as possible.

comm units. In order to stop the growing delirium, the heroes might have to fight off those other guests (including a celebrated champion of the vicious sport of brutaris) who have been transformed into hideous abominations!

## THE PENUMBRA PROTOCOL
**By Jenny Jarzabski**
*Starfinder Adventure Path* #11, Levels 9–10

Infected with a sickness that threatens to turn them into twisted sadists, the heroes travel to the city of Cuvacara on the planet Verces to find Eclipse Innovations, the tech company that created the virtual concierge. They soon discover that this sinister company plans to release a new social media app that will corrupt the entire city in the same fashion as New Elysium. Surviving attacks from corporate assassins, the heroes can shut down the app's servers and discover the location of the company's hidden underground base on the planet's Darkside. Individuals who seem to have willingly undergone transformation lurk within and now protect the facility with their lives. After confronting the charismatic executive in charge and learning about Dr. Lestana Gragant—the corrupted scientist who created the signal—the heroes find they are now trapped on the Shadow Plane!

## HEART OF NIGHT
**By Saif Ansari**
*Starfinder Adventure Path* #12, Levels 11–12

The only hope of returning to the Material Plane is to find and destroy the twisted scientist responsible for engineering the transformative signal. At a creepy spacedock controlled by worshipers of Zon-Kuthon, the PCs are able to retrieve a shadow version of their own starship, which they can use to return to New Elysium's asteroid. Fighting disturbing vessels piloted by velstracs who want to flay them alive, the heroes arrive at a twisted place where the moans and screams of unseen beings echo through unfamiliar halls. At the center of this web, the heroes confront Dr. Gragant herself, who has been transformed into a unique outsider through her experimentation with pain and pleasure. Using her notes and partially living machinery, the PCs can cure themselves of their own corruption (if they wish) and find a way home!

# THE DIASPORA STRAIN

## ADVANCEMENT TRACK

"The Diaspora Strain" is designed for four characters.

 The PCs begin this adventure at 7th level.

 The PCs should reach 8th level as they explore the tunnels under the resort.

 The PCs should be 9th level by the end of the adventure.

## ADVENTURE BACKGROUND

Several decades ago, after watching her parents die in agony from painful illnesses, Dr. Lestana Gragant began her work to eliminate pain in the galaxy. Her childhood loss fueled her ascent through the medical world. She gained a reputation for thorough research into ways to control and mitigate pain, but she failed to create practical applications from her work. Then the Swarm attacked the Pact Worlds and the Veskarium.

Eclipse Innovations, a Vercite firm, hired Dr. Gragant to create military technology that would inure soldiers to pain. The company purchased asteroid D-334H, an enormous rock in the Diaspora that Ulrikka Clanholdings had mined out over 15 years before, and built a facility within the asteroid's tunnels. Eclipse pressured Gragant for results, and she turned to unethical practices to speed up her research. Corporate security forces provided her with captured pirates as test subjects, and the once-idealistic doctor took the first steps on her path into darkness when she persuaded herself that, in the pursuit of her noble goal, the life and suffering of a criminal didn't matter.

Dr. Gragant became convinced that the key to success was turning pain into pleasure. However, doing so would require Dr. Gragant to escape the constraints of science by dabbling in magic. As Eclipse Innovations' demands became threats to cut her funding, Dr. Gragant used her unproven technomagical theories on herself. The result was a magical cascade that drew portions of her lab into the Shadow Plane, killing most of her assistants and test subjects. Eclipse covered up the incident, sealed what was left of the lab, and shelved the research, thinking Lestana Gragant dead. They were wrong.

The experiment transformed Dr. Gragant into a supernatural being, a fiend without a trace of compassion or empathy. Trapped in the shadow version of her facility, she hungered for pain. For over a decade, she honed her powers, learned to influence the Material Plane, and found allies among fiends similar to herself. She corrupted a few space pirates and other explorers of D-334H in this way but, mystically tied to the asteroid, her reach was severely limited.

That limitation ended when Eclipse Innovations, through several shell corporations and back channels, sold D-334H to Paradise Resorts. Paradise planned to build a vacation facility where the rich could be pampered while experiencing the Diaspora up close. New Elysium, as the resort was to be called, broke ground on the asteroid 5 years ago. Dr. Gragant watched and waited, working subtle corruptions on the administrators and workers, curious to see where this flurry of activity might lead. Her patience paid off. Gragant influenced Paradise Resort's managers to approach Eclipse, whom she blamed for her losses and transformation, and incorporate some of the corporation's technology into the asteroid's automated facilities. Soon, an Eclipse Innovations executive named Kaeon Rhyse arrived at New Elysium to facilitate this project.

Over the next year, Gragant corrupted Rhyse completely. In turn, Rhyse brought Gragant more potential converts from Eclipse Innovations' home offices. Most of these disciples returned to Verces, allowing Gragant to slowly gain control over her former employer, and now the entire corporation serves her interests. Most recently, Eclipse has upgraded New Elysium's automated systems to interface with visitors' comm units and personal computing devices through a program called Keys to Elysium.

This "virtual concierge" program is actually part of Gragant's plan to turn pain into pleasure throughout the galaxy. While the program puts control of resort amenities in the guests' hands, it also carries a shadow signal that amplifies Gragant's powers of corruption, allowing her to manipulate users of the program even more efficiently and quickly than she has so many others on the asteroid. If she can successfully subvert the wills of a large group of people in a short period of time, Gragant has the means to extend her influence to other worlds!

## THE INVITATION

The Signal of Screams Adventure Path starts with the PCs receiving an invitation to a vacation facility called New Elysium. The resort's new social manager, Filip Kallsner, has invited significant persons from regions all across known space to participate in an exclusive debut of the Keys to Elysium virtual concierge. The text of this invitation is presented in the handout at the top of page 5.

The player characters might receive this invitation for any one of several reasons, and it should feel like a reward for past deeds, even if you are beginning this campaign with new characters. Each PC could receive her own invitation, or the PCs could receive one as a group. Several rooms can be offered, as the size of the party requires. Some suggestions for why the PCs get invited to New Elysium follow. Use them as written, or change them to fit the backstories of your player characters. Paradise Resorts invites all sorts of individuals to the resort for a variety of reasons.

**After the Aeon Throne:** Player characters who survived the Against the Aeon Throne Adventure Path likely earned renown for their role in those events. If the PCs kept a low profile in their struggle against the Azlanti Star Empire, a friend or contact, such as Cedona or another member of the Stewards, might recommend the group for the guest list out of gratitude. The person who makes this vacation possible has no idea of the truth behind New Elysium; they want only to give the PCs the gift of well-earned relaxation.

**Celebrity Calls:** Paradise Resorts wants celebrities to experience and spread the word about New Elysium and its new system of automation. The PCs are well-known individuals, especially if any character in the group has the icon theme. Similar distinction in other fields, such as being

## FELICITATIONS!

PARADISE RESORTS IS PROUD TO OFFER YOU A COMPLEMENTARY THREE WEEK STAY AT NEW ELYSIUM, THE DIASPORA-BASED LUXURY RESORT FOR THE DISCERNING VACATIONER. PAMPER YOURSELF WITH OUR SUMPTUOUS GUEST SERVICES, INCLUDING BODY WRAPS, MASSAGES, AND MUD FACIALS! RELAX IN ONE OF OUR TWO POOLS, COMPLETE WITH ARTIFICIAL WATERFALLS! INDULGE IN THE FINEST FOOD FROM ACROSS THE GALAXY! AND SO MUCH MORE, ALL AT YOUR FINGERTIPS WITH OUR BRAND-NEW KEYS TO ELYSIUM VIRTUAL CONCIERGE DOWNLOADED DIRECTLY INTO YOUR COMM UNIT!

IN ADDITION TO PICKING UP THE TAB FOR YOUR ROOM, MEALS, AND ANY OTHER SERVICES YOU INDULGE IN, PARADISE RESORTS IS ALSO HOLDING A GRAND GALA FOR ALL GUESTS ON THE SECOND NIGHT OF YOUR STAY. MEET AND MINGLE WITH YOUR PEERS, AND MAYBE MAKE A NEW FRIEND!

DISCLAIMER: PARADISE RESORTS IS NOT RESPONSIBLE FOR EXTRA FEES YOU MIGHT INCUR, SUCH AS FOR EXPENSIVE CONSUMABLES, TOP-SHELF INTOXICANTS, PORTABLE GEAR, AUGMENTATIONS, AND SIMILAR GOODS.

SIGNAL OF SCREAMS

CAMPAIGN OUTLINE

THE DIASPORA STRAIN

PART 1: TWILIGHT IN ELYSIUM

PART 2: WAKING NIGHTMARES

PART 3: PARTING THE GLOOM

CORRUPTED BY SHADOWS

HORROR CAMPAIGNS

ALIEN ARCHIVES

CODEX OF WORLDS

a prominent scholar or an eminent explorer, can also result in an invitation. Other New Elysium guests include a software entrepreneur and several sports figures, and any or all the PCs might have similar cultural appeal and anticipated value as word-of-mouth advertisers.

**Patron's Gift:** The PCs recently performed a massive favor or job for a wealthy patron and, in addition to whatever payment they received, get put on the guest list for New Elysium's gala event. The task the PCs performed was likely dangerous or perilous and their patron assures them that they "earned a vacation." This patron is unaware of what is about to happen on the resort.

**Sweepstakes Winners:** To attract a full house of participants and attain a broader spectrum of attendees, New Elysium held a system-wide sweepstakes for numerous guest slots. One or more of the PCs might have filled out an entry during previous adventures. Guess who won? Alternatively, a business associate, friend, or relative might have entered the contest and won, but can't go. That acquaintance gives the ticket to the PCs. Either way, a winning ticket allows for the entire group to enjoy a free vacation at New Elysium.

**The Unconnected Group:** The previous hooks assume the PCs have preexisting relationships and share a starship. Although such connections make the group more cohesive and possibly deepen the horror that develops, prior relationships aren't required. In such a case, each PC has received his own invitation to New Elysium (involving any of the reasons listed above). At the start of the adventure, they are being flown to the resort as passengers on a Ringworks Sentinel (see the inside covers). They might even be flying with NPCs they will later work with or oppose (see Key Characters on page 6).

If you begin the campaign this way, you will need to alter **Event 1** to make the encounter fairer, perhaps by reducing the number of Diasporan Raiders by one or replacing all the enemy

vessels with BMC Maulers (*Starfinder Core Rulebook* 314). Also, the PCs will have to convince the Sentinel's normal crew to let them take over the ship and answer the distress call. However, this approach has the benefit of essentially isolating the PCs on New Elysium when things start to get bad; they can't just get in their vessel and fly away. In this case, the group should still create a tier 8 starship they can use later (see **Event 16**).

## BUILDING A STARSHIP

The PCs should begin this adventure with their own starship, either from their previous adventures or, if your players are creating new 7th-level characters, a new tier 7 starship they collectively create. As the campaign progresses, the PCs will have opportunities to improve their starship and customize it further.

## ARMOR AND WEAPONS ON NEW ELYSIUM

If any of the PCs ask about the resort's policy on armor and weapons, let them know they won't be expected to turn over any of their gear, though they will be asked to safely stow most of their armaments in their guest accommodations. The Diaspora can be a dangerous place, and while the resort has its own security detail, having competent fighters such as the PCs around might put some of the other guests at ease. However, carrying large and obvious weapons and wearing heavy armor is generally frowned on and considered tacky.

## RESEARCHING THE RESORT

A PC who succeeds at a DC 20 check to recall knowledge with Culture or an appropriate Profession skill (corporate professional, for instance), can learn more about New Elysium and Paradise Resorts. The PCs already know that Paradise Resorts owns New Elysium and paid for them to go on this trip. Those who succeed at the check also identify Paradise Resorts as a small corporation specializing in unusual vacation locations. The company owns several tourist centers, including Cloud Nine, a floating campground in the clouds of Bretheda, and Utopiana, a beachside hotel on Castrovel. Paradise Resorts has a good reputation among its customers, and it's moderately profitable. The company has a wide variety of partners that offer services and goods vacationers might desire while visiting their resorts.

## PART 1: TWILIGHT IN ELYSIUM

The Signal of Screams Adventure Path truly begins as the PCs approach the part of the Diaspora where New Elysium's asteroid floats.

## KEY CHARACTERS

The following nonplayer characters are important to this adventure. Unless stated otherwise, these people are celebrities invited to attend New Elysium's reopening. It is central to the growing horror of the adventure that the PCs develop a relationship with some of these NPCs, as later on, they will become foes or die according to the needs of the story.

You might want to assign a note card to each NPC and record their interactions with and feelings about each PC on it. You can use similar cards to track NPCs you add to the scenario if the PCs meet people not mentioned here. Most interactions with these characters will consist of roleplaying, until noted otherwise. If the PCs want to attempt any checks against these NPCs, you can assume the base DC for such checks is 22 and adjust it as needed. Most NPCs have a starting attitude of indifferent. However, all resort staff members start as friendly to the PCs.

### NEW ELYSIUM STAFF

Almost 30 people are usually required to take care of guests and maintain the facility, supplementing the resort's automated services (see New Elysium Features on page 11). During this reopening, there are far fewer guests than normal and the number of staff members has been reduced accordingly. Unnamed minor personnel rotate between various jobs. When not working, many of the staff can be found mingling with guests. Among the resort personnel, only Kaeon Rhyse knows what is truly going on at New Elysium. All other workers believe the reopening event is a marketing strategy. They have no inkling of Dr. Gragant's shadow carrier signal and are simply additional test subjects. The prominent staff members in the adventure are listed below.

DR. SIDRANI LOMINN

**Filip Kallsner** (N male halfling envoy) is New Elysium's host and social manager. He oversees the hosting staff, such as those working in lounges and restaurants. Tall for a halfling, Filip dresses well in dark business attire or formal wear, sometimes of unusual subtle hues. He's easy to like, genuine and friendly, smooth without being slimy, and accommodating without being obsequious.

**Kaeon Rhyse** (LE male verthani technomancer) is the Eclipse Innovations executive mentioned in the Adventure Background. Kaeon makes only a brief appearance in this adventure and will be further detailed in the next adventure, "The Penumbra Protocol."

**Kane Zaphol** (LN male human soldier), New Elysium's security specialist, commands the resort's security squads and starship patrols. He is fit and looks the part of a proper, groomed military officer. Although he follows the rules and maintains decorum, he's arrogant and authoritarian.

**Rhissona Avran** (LE female reptoid master) works under Dr. Lominn (detailed below) as an augmentation specialist. Rhissona disguises herself as a verthani of the Augmented caste, gaunt with cropped blue hair. She's courteous but pretends to be more comfortable in her job than in social situations.

**Dr. Sidrani Lominn** (LN female human) is the physician who supervises New Elysium's spa and medical facilities. She's second to Filip Kallsner when it comes to managerial authority. The doctor is usually wearing a light-colored lab coat over business attire in neutral shades, wearing her dark hair pinned back. Dr. Lominn maintains a professional demeanor while attempting to remain approachable, and has a sincere desire to help and care for guests within facility rules.

**Vorilynn Wreyas** (NG female half-elf mystic), a retired Xenowarden, got the job overseeing care for Green Fields and New Elysium's other flora largely because she is a friend of the Kallsner family. Vorilynn (whom Filip calls Vori) works at New Elysium in order to gain access to the resort's amenities. Vori wraps her willowy frame in robes and often leaves her long silver hair loose or tied in a bun.

### ABSALOM BUZZBLADES

After winning the latest championship, members of the Absalom Buzzblades, a popular team known for its dominance of the gladiatorial sport, brutaris, were invited to New Elysium. Only six of the team's 13 first-string members could make it, as the others are still recuperating from their last match. Brutaris is played on a wide field with changeable obstacles, goals, and a spiked ball called the brutaris. Players who run and handle the ball are called backs, and players who engage in most of the conflict, protecting the backs, are called forwards.

**Beryldor Rendrumm** (N male dwarf soldier) is a strong young forward with close-cropped red hair and a trim beard. He's jolly and distractible. The others call him "the new kid."

**Kofehsu Tasa Ni Raeda Saeru of Clan Rishnu** (LN male kasatha technomancer) is a lithe and fast rear-back. He likes to talk strategy and philosophy but doesn't tolerate foolish or disrespectful behavior directed at him or his teammates.

**Lomer** (LE agender android solarian) is a center-back, short and solidly built, with curly hair and skin the color of bronze with copper accents. They are sharp-witted, have a dark sense of humor, and often follows Virlae's lead.

**Virlae Nilufeh** (LE female korasha lashunta operative) is a young fast-back or "winger." She is friendly but a bit egotistical. Of the Buzzblades, she is the first to be affected by New Elysium's ambient corruption.

**Yazeloya Golkami** (LN female vesk soldier), the most massive and renowned of the Buzzblades, is the team's notorious number 13, a lock-back or "demoralizer." Yazeloya has a fearsome on-field reputation, but in person, she's gregarious and respectful, often displaying physical affection, especially to those who show courage and strength. However, she has no regard for cowards.

**Zidhil Quorin** (LN male human soldier), the second largest Buzzblade, is an older forward. He is nearing retirement, with oiled black wavy hair and beard. He's reserved and observant. Other Buzzblades look up to him.

## OTHER GUESTS

Several of the resort's approximately 50 other guests play a significant role in the adventure.

**Cthesa** (N female shirren) is a travel writer known for harsh but fair criticism of vacation sites across the Pact Worlds. Paradise Resorts invited her for obvious reasons. She is outgoing and venturesome, and has an athletic build that accommodates her adventurous spirit. Her antennae tend to twitch when she gets excited about something.

**Indigo-13** (NG female android), personal attendant and bodyguard to Romi (detailed below), has a feminine-leaning appearance and affect. She has pale skin with blue accents and blue fiber-optic hair that can illuminate and change color to emphasize her mood. Indigo is outgoing and tries to influence Romi to step outside their narrow comfort zone. However, if anyone threatens her or Romi, Indigo-13 can be ruthless.

**Romi** (NG agender android) is a software mogul from Aballon famous for consulting on personal interface solutions. Paradise Resorts invited Romi for professional feedback on Keys to Elysium. The android abstains from downloading or using the virtual concierge, but also keeps an eye on how other guests interface with the program. Romi is an intellectually curious android who displays very few emotional responses, relying on their personal attendant and bodyguard Indigo-13 to navigate social events. They are hairless, with ebony skin,

and wear plain, practical, loose-fitting clothing, sometimes going barefoot.

**Tok "Crower" Nahgiz** (NE male ysoki), a holovid streamer infamous for broadcasting tawdry material, is here because he "won" a ticket by getting his audience to enter the sweepstakes mentioned on page 5 using his name. While this was technically against the rules of the contest, Paradise Resorts didn't wish to anger Tok's fan base, so they cut a deal with the ysoki, allowing him to attend as long as he doesn't broadcast his stay live. Tok has black fur and wears eyewear that includes tiny cameras, which he uses to record everything. He plans to edit the footage later for an extended documentary.

## UNWANTED GUEST

A cantor (see page 60) named Teodhor has infiltrated the resort from the Shadow Plane. One of the many velstracs—outsiders native to the Shadow Plane who feed on fear and pain—Dr. Gragant swayed to her side over the years, Teodhor stalks the corridors, using his nightmare powers to further corrupt the resort's guests. Teodhor has biometric security clearance (see New Elysium Features on page 11), but he moves around only at night, using Stealth and the *shadow body* spell to avoid detection. During most of the adventure, he avoids confronting anyone, including the PCs, but they might spot him more than once.

## EVENT 1: BRUTARIS DISTRESS (CR 9)

When the PCs arrive in the sector of the Diaspora near New Elysium, they intercept a distress call.

---

"Shuttle Goal Runner to New Elysium security! We're under attack! Request immediate assistance!"

The response is quick. "Acknowledged, Goal Runner. We're on our way. Hang in there."

"They'll never get here in time, Buzzblades!" an unknown person with a gravelly voice interjects. "Give it up, and we'll go easy on ya." The transmission ends with laughter and hooting from what must be other ships in the area.

---

A PC who is a sports fan or who succeeds at a DC 12 Culture check recognizes the name "Buzzblades" as the champion brutaris team of Absalom Station. The *Goal Runner* must be the team's transport vehicle.

**Starship Combat:** The PCs' ship is close enough to quickly come to the *Goal Runner*'s aid. Three other small ships harry the shuttle, hooting and taunting over the communications channel. It is easy for the PCs to determine that low on shields and firepower, the *Goal Runner* can't hold out until the New Elysium security ships arrive.

As the PCs approach, place their ship on one side of the map, approximately 25 to 30 hexes from the *Goal Runner* and the three Diasporan Raiders, pirate fighters not associated with the Free Captains. The intervening space is cluttered with small asteroids. Using tokens to represent these hazards, place 20 asteroids on the map, with no two in adjacent hexes. A starship can fly through a space containing an asteroid, but the pilot must succeed at a DC 25 Piloting check or clip the asteroid, dealing 1d10 damage to her starship in a random arc. A starship can shoot at an asteroid, which is considered to have AC 5 and TL 5 and is destroyed when dealt 5 Hull Points of damage.

When combat begins, two of the Diasporan Raiders move to engage the PCs' vessel, correctly believing it to be the larger threat. The third continues to harass the *Goal Runner*, which enters the field of asteroids to try and escape the battle. Though the shuttle is fleeing, Yazeloya takes on the role of gunner and fires the laser net at the pirate chasing her ship. Both the pirates and the *Goal Runner* have taken some damage to their shields, as noted in their stat blocks.

If you like, a player can roll for Yazeloya's gunnery checks using the bonus listed below. The PCs can also encourage the *Goal Runner*'s crew to perform specific actions over their comm units. The brutaris players are more than willing to accept the PCs' suggestions, but if you think a course of action sounds risky or unusual, the PC who suggested it must succeed at a DC 20 Diplomacy or Intimidate check (which takes no starships action) for the *Goal Runner* to enact it.

During the combat, the pirates taunt and annoy their targets. If the PCs and the *Goal Runner* do well in the fight, the Buzzblades (especially Yazeloya) cheer their rescuers and return the pirates' gibes. If the players haven't already done so, Yazeloya might recommend the PCs and the *Goal Runner* team up and focus fire on a single pirate fighter. Any pirate fighter reduced to half its Hull Points or fewer flees. Once two pirates retreat or are defeated, the third also runs for it. The *Goal Runner* remains as long as the PCs' ship does.

At the start of the fifth round, New Elysium security arrives in the form of two Ringworks Sentinels (see inside front cover) which enter the map on the same edge the PCs' vessel started from. Any remaining pirates flee at this point. See Development below for the pirates' parting words.

## DIASPORAN RAIDERS (3) — TIER 4

Tiny fighter

**Speed** 10; **Maneuverability** good (turn 1); **Drift** 2
**AC** 21; **TL** 20
**HP** 40 each; **DT** —; **CT** 8
**Shields** medium 100 (currently 86; forward 21, port 22, starboard 22, aft 21)
**Attack (Forward)** high explosive missile launcher (4d8), light particle beam (6d6)
**Attack (Aft)** linked flak throwers (6d4)
**Power Core** Arcus Heavy (130 PCU); **Drift Engine** Signal Booster; **Systems** basic medium-range sensors, extra light weapon mount (aft), mk 3 duonode computer, mk 5 armor, mk 5 defenses; **Expansion Bays** none
**Modifiers** +3 to any two checks per round, +2 Computers (sensors only), +1 Piloting; **Complement** 2

### CREW
**Gunner** Computers +12 (4 ranks), gunnery +8
**Pilot** Piloting +16 (4 ranks), gunnery +8

## GOAL RUNNER — TIER 4

Small shuttle

**Speed** 10; **Maneuverability** perfect (turn 0); **Drift** 2
**AC** 20; **TL** 19
**HP** 40; **DT** —; **CT** 8
**Shields** medium 120 (currently 80; forward 20, port 20, starboard 20, aft 20)
**Attack (Forward)** light particle beam (3d6)
**Attack (Turret)** laser net (2d6)
**Power Core** Arcus Heavy (130 PCU); **Drift Engine** Signal Booster; **Systems** basic medium-range sensors, crew quarters (good), extra light weapon mount (turret), mk 2 duonode computer, mk 5 armor, mk 5 defenses; **Expansion Bays** guest quarters (2 good), recreation suite (gym)
**Modifiers** +2 to any two checks per round, +2 Computers (sensors only), +2 Piloting; **Complement** 3 (plus guests)

### CREW
**Engineer** Computers +12 (4 ranks), Engineering +12 (4 ranks)
**Gunners (2)** Engineering +8 (4 ranks), gunnery +8
**Pilot** Piloting +17 (4 ranks), gunnery +8

DIASPORAN RAIDER

**Development:** If the pirates disable both the *Goal Runner* and the PCs' ship, they don't have enough time to board either vessel before New Elysium security arrives. The pirates flee from the Sentinels, who don't bother chasing after them, prioritizing the safety of the guests. The Sentinels tow any disabled vessels back to New Elysium.

Either way, when the pirates leave, read or paraphrase the following.

---

A message arrives from one of the New Elysium ships. "Guest vessel, thank you for your assistance. Please proceed to New Elysium. We'll handle the situation from here."

"Rot on that rock, maggots," answers a scratchy-voiced pirate. "May you join our mates what haunt its innards."

---

If New Elysium security doesn't have to tow the PCs' vessel or the *Goal Runner* to the resort, and the PCs didn't disable any of the pirate ships, the Sentinels give chase. Ultimately, the Sentinels capture a pirate ship, giving the PCs a chance to later interrogate one of the pirates (see **Event 2**). Neither the New Elysium security force nor the Buzzblades know anything about the pirates' final cryptic remark. The security crew has no authority to authorize any recompense for damage to the PCs' vessel or guarantee salvage rights for any disabled pirate ship, but they assure the PCs that such matters can be discussed at the resort.

**Story Award:** If the PCs survive the encounter with the pirate ships, award them 6,400 XP. If the PCs managed to rescue the *Goal Runner* before it is disabled, award them an additional 2,400 XP.

## ARRIVAL AT NEW ELYSIUM

Shortly after the battle with the pirates, the PCs arrive at New Elysium. Read or paraphrase the following.

---

New Elysium's docking area is a multiarmed facility on the side of an enormous asteroid. Above it, built into the space-borne rock, is a sleek structure with countless windows, as well as a huge, clear dome. A computerized message plays from the comm unit.

"Welcome! Relax, and our automated docking system will guide you in. You'll be ready to disembark shortly."

True to the message, docking takes only a few moments. A mechanical clank and a sharp hiss accompany the station's airlock passageway linking to the ship.

"You are now ready to disembark. Welcome to New Elysium, a plane unto itself among the stars, untouched by sorrow."

---

The resort's airlock opens onto a short, polished hallway that, in turn, leads to a wider corridor that slopes gently upward. If the PCs helped the *Goal Runner*, they see the Absalom Buzzblades as they disembark; the *Goal Runner*'s three-person crew remains aboard the shuttle and soon

departs from the resort if the shuttle is still able to do so. The Buzzblades are grateful, especially Yazeloya, who gives a hearty embrace of friendship to any PC who gets within her reach. In the event that the PCs ignored the *Goal Runner*'s distress call, the Buzzblades arrive well after the PCs do, and any interaction with them occurs later.

In either case, Filip Kallsner comes to welcome the PCs, walking with a departing Kaeon Rhyse. Read or paraphrase the following.

---

Four people stride down the corridor's slight slope. One is a striking verthani man with black eyes, slickly styled dark hair, and an expensive-looking charcoal suit accented with violet matching the illumination on his cybernetic right arm. The other is a halfling of athletic proportions, with conventionally handsome tan skin, curly hair, and trimmed sideburns. He wears dark business attire with a subtle crimson hue. The other two people, both verthani women dressed in black microcord armor, are clearly security personnel or bodyguards. They stand back as the two suited men come closer.

---

Filip and Kaeon greet the PCs and the Buzzblades, although Filip is friendlier by far. Both men praise any action the PCs took to defend the *Goal Runner*. Kaeon then announces he must depart for Verces, and after shaking Filip's hand and wishing everyone a fine stay, he and his guards proceed down a side corridor to a waiting starship. If asked who Kaeon is, Filip refers to him as an executive for one of New Elysium's partners who "... of course, appreciates his privacy."

### A Handsome Reward

Filip again thanks the PCs for intervening on behalf of the *Goal Runner*, provided they did, and apologizes for the trouble and dangers inherent to New Elysium's location. He assures the group that Paradise Resorts is more than willing to see to repairs on the *Goal Runner* and the PCs' starship, and further offers to facilitate ship upgrades during that time (Filip offers these refitting services even if the PCs didn't aid the *Goal Runner*), allowing the PCs to have their ship upgraded to tier 8 before the end of the adventure (see page 38). Filip also insists the PCs be further compensated for their deeds. With a few gestures on a datapad, he sends each PC a 5,000-credit gift allowance for use in New Elysium's shops or via infosphere with one of Paradise Resorts' many partners. Effectively, this sum is cash, due to the broad array of items the PCs can buy with it, limited only by your discretion. It is also transferable to banks or other financial institutions for full value.

If the PCs ask about salvage rights to any pirate ship they disabled, Filip assures them the miscreants carried nothing of value, saying, "Otherwise, why would they turn to a life of crime?" If they press him, Filip begs the PCs to let him take care of such "tedious business" during their resort stay, suggesting he will notify them of any developments.

SIGNAL OF SCREAMS

CAMPAIGN OUTLINE

THE DIASPORA STRAIN

PART 1: TWILIGHT IN ELYSIUM

PART 2: WAKING NIGHTMARES

PART 3: PARTING THE GLOOM

CORRUPTED BY SHADOWS

HORROR CAMPAIGNS

ALIEN ARCHIVES

CODEX OF WORLDS

## GETTING THE APP

After the exchange of niceties and appropriate rewards, Filip invites those present to follow him. During the walk, he introduces the Keys to Elysium virtual concierge. Read or paraphrase the following.

---

"One reason you've all been invited to our little resort is to be the first to experience an upgrade to our amenities," says Filip. "We have maximized guest comfort by way of software integration. Our Keys to Elysium app is your personal concierge, putting everything we offer at your command with a touch or a word. Here."

Using his datapad, Filip calls up a 3-D icon shaped like a silver key and flicks it.

---

Each of the PCs' comm units asks permission to accept the download of a new program.

---

Filip smiles. "There. Now, anything you want here at the resort is as close as your comm unit. Your free stay is predicated on you using the app and allowing it to send us relevant data. You can also use it to send us feedback in real time and, if you like, anonymously. We're sure you'll love it. You can give the virtual personality any name you wish and it will respond, though it defaults to 'Keys.' The app is voice-activated, so simply ask for whatever you need, like so."

"Keys, please allow our guests to choose their rooms."

The program chimes pleasantly. "Yes, Filip," responds a cheerful, androgynous voice.

---

The app then offers the PCs their choice of rooms, presenting them various configurations, such as suites or individual lodgings, as well as opportunities to reside together or have accommodations close to one another. It also prompts them to configure any settings, such as the name it will respond to and whether it should respond with text or voice. For more on what the program provides (as well as its unintended effects), see Keys to Elysium below.

If the Buzzblades are present, they confer about room choices for a bit and settle on a pair of adjoining suites, similar to the quarters they shared on the *Goal Runner*. Filip then leads the guests into the main facility (see Into Green Fields on page 11).

## KEYS TO ELYSIUM

The Keys to Elysium app is a personal, virtual concierge. Using Keys to Elysium, guests can order or schedule anything the resort offers, connect with facilities, and control features such as hot tubs or the air conditioning and lighting in their rooms. A user can interact with the app through voice commands or contextual menus. In play, PCs need to only state what they want, and the app does the rest. The app can speak in a variety of languages and adopt a number of different virtual personalities.

**Installation:** As part of accepting their free stay on New Elysium, the PCs agreed to install and use Keys to Elysium. If a guest logs out of the app, staff members check in on that person quickly and remind him of the terms and conditions of the invitation. Once installed, logging out or even deleting the app doesn't stop the corruption growing within the PCs (see below). Dr. Gragant's shadow signal is still being broadcast throughout the facility; the app only amplifies her power.

**Features:** In addition to amenity controls and a service-based interface, the app allows guests to tag other users as friends (or block other guests as unwanted company), communicate instantly with one another, and so on. These features aren't anything new to modern comm units, but Keys to Elysium contextualizes it all relative to the resort and its features. The app also includes an interactive map of the public areas of the resort, and this map can be customized to show where friends are located.

**Settings:** The app allows guests to customize how the app is used, allowing them to manage alerts, personal tracking, and vocal feedback; identify people as blocked or friends; and even set proximity alerts to signal a user when a blocked person or a friend is nearby. A user can clear data, send usage statistics and feedback, and set the app's contextual guidance from full tutorial mode to no guidance at all. By default, Keys to Elysium has accessed each PC's personal information for use in personalized resort ads, although this permission can be turned off in the app's settings. A PC who succeeds at a DC 20 Computers check can find an "About" dialog box in the settings that includes a user agreement and privacy policy and reveals Eclipse Innovations as the software's manufacturer.

The app is set to automatically update, but this setting isn't obvious (a successful DC 31 Computers check is required to find it). If a PC attempts to shut off auto-updating, the app warns that doing so is a violation of the guest agreement that granted the PCs their free vacation. Doing so anyway attracts attention from staff, who seek out the guest and remind her of the app's terms and conditions.

**Curse:** Keys to Elysium infects a comm unit's firmware after 48 hours of use (even if the user logs out of the app, but its automatic updating must still be on), turning the comm unit into a cursed item that compels its owner to keep it nearby. Most users don't notice this compulsion, since desiring to keep one's comm unit handy is not abnormal. The curse also compels the user to keep the app installed and stay logged in, but once again, this compulsion goes unnoticed by anyone who might consider this to be normal behavior. (Most people don't log out of their comm unit apps.) However, someone in possession of a cursed comm unit treats the DC for saving throws against phantasms (see page 21) as 3 higher and the DCs for contracting shadow corruption (see page 42) as 1 higher for a good-aligned character, 2 higher for a neutral-character, and 3 higher for an evil-aligned character.

**Analysis:** Analyzing Keys to Elysium's software (a violation of the user agreement) requires a successful DC 31 Computers check that takes 1 hour (a PC can take 20 on this check). On a failure by 5 or more, the app alerts the staff of the attempt. A success on this check reveals the app is hybrid technology, albeit nothing unusual, and only hinting at the curse. Succeeding at the check by 5 or more after the app has cursed the comm unit shows that the program has altered parts of the device's firmware to receive a constant, low-grade signal. The signal can be traced with a successful DC 36 Computers check, originating from somewhere below the resort in the old Ulrikka Clanholdings mines. See Part 2 for more details on this signal.

The curse is difficult to detect since it is hidden from spells like *detect magic* and *identify*. The spell *detect magic* doesn't detect the curse, but if a PC casts *identify*, she can attempt a DC 36 Mysticism check to locate the curse (but doesn't benefit from the spell's usual +10 insight bonus). If a PC finds the curse, she can attempt to analyze it with the *identify* spell as normal (an additional DC 36 Mysticism check) and benefits from that spell's normal insight bonus. Taking 20 on either of these checks is impossible, as there is no outside information about this curse. Successfully identifying the curse not only reveals its effects (see above) but also allows the PC to learn that the magic is tied to the Shadow Plane and determine how the curse might be removed (see below).

**Removal:** The only way to remove the curse is to wipe the comm unit's firmware with a successful DC 30 Computers check. Casting *dispel magic* on the cursed comm unit grants a +4 circumstance bonus to this check. Casting *remove affliction* and succeeding at a DC 24 caster level check suppresses the curse long enough that completely restoring the comm unit to factory settings requires only a successful DC 20 Computers check. Once the curse has been identified, a PC who succeeds at a DC 25 Mysticism check recognizes that these spells can help, but a PC can use only one of these spells on a single comm unit at a time. Once a comm unit is cleansed this way, the Keys to Elysium app is no longer installed on it, but neither is any other program the PC might have installed. Removing the curse from a comm unit doesn't remove any shadow corruption the PC who was using it might have contracted.

## RESEARCH INTO ECLIPSE INNOVATIONS

PCs who investigate the program's settings might discover the name of Eclipse Innovations. A PC who succeeds at a DC 25 Culture or appropriate Profession skill (corporate professional, for instance) recognizes Eclipse Innovations as a research company specializing in diverse technological and magitech inquiry and application. The firm is based in the Vercite city of Cuvacara. Nothing about its public information mentions New Elysium or the Keys to Elysium program, instead previewing (in an attempt to build up buzz) a "social media solution" called Penumbra, which will be available very soon. Eclipse is a large business with an average reputation, neither virtuous nor scandalous. The verthani Kaeon Rhyse isn't mentioned anywhere obvious on Eclipse's infosphere page, but a PC who succeeds at a DC 30 Computers or Perception check while perusing the infosphere discovers that he is the executive director of software development.

## INTO GREEN FIELDS

After walking through the dock hallway (area **A1**), the PCs emerge in the resort's park, Green Fields (area **A2**). Read or paraphrase the following, which assumes an early evening arrival.

---

An extensive domed area opens ahead, replete with smells of fresh water, grass, and honeysuckle. The dome overhead mimics a partially cloudy sunset sky, lighting a broad meadow interspersed with trees, a creek, and a pond. Other guests lounge or play in the park. To the rear of the park is a gigantic cliff around a cave, which has a waterfall on its back wall.

Filip turns and smiles. "Welcome to Green Fields, the resort's park, with an Absalom-standard day-to-night ratio. Our asteroid rotates slowly, so the sun isn't visible through the dome during our night phase, but the River Between is. Green Fields has everything, from swimming to a trail we call the Loop. Even a bar in the Grotto there! Traversing the Loop takes you all the way around the facility with a spectacular view the whole time!"

He laughs. "Sorry, my enthusiasm is running away with me. Keys to Elysium can provide you details on our amenities. You can also use it to contact me or other resort staff. If there's nothing else, I'll leave you to enjoy your evening."

---

With that, Filip nods and leaves the PCs (and the Buzzblades if they are present) to their own devices. As Filip passes, he greets the half-elf Vorilynn Wreyas, who is noticeably performing gardening tasks. If any of the PCs appear interested in the resort's flora, Vorilynn hails them and talks effusively about the authenticity of New Elysium's natural settings. Each person's Keys to Elysium reminds them about the opening gala, which is scheduled to occur at 6:00 P.M. the next day. The program then starts a celebratory countdown.

### NEW ELYSIUM FEATURES

The PCs have free run of the resort before the party.

New Elysium has three floors—a main floor, a lower floor that includes staff facilities, and a lodging floor for guest

FILIP KALLSNER

and staff rooms. A side view of the resort can be found on page 32. Unlike the dock hallway (area **A1**), much of the resort is carved from the asteroid to give it a natural look. However, these walls are reinforced, and interior structures are modern composites as hard as steel. The resort has the following features.

**Structure:** New Elysium is built to simulate a series of buildings with walkways and courtyards open to the sky. The ceiling and walls of open areas are clear composite, beyond which is vacuum. However, these structures either project holographic images of sunny daytime scenes or the actual Diasporan sky, in which the River Between can often be seen. Guests can manipulate nearby viewing areas so the actual exterior can be seen at any time, effectively creating personal windows into space. The ceilings inside buildings on the main and lower floors and in the facilities section of the lower floor, are around 20 feet high. The ceiling in "outside" areas is 40 feet high.

**Doors:** Throughout the resort's guest sections are automatic sliding doors that open when approached and close behind. Doors to private rooms or staff facilities can be and usually are locked with good locks that can be bypassed with a successful DC 30 Engineering check or a successful DC 33 Computers check using a hacking kit. Keys to Elysium allows the PCs to open their private rooms. Staff members use biometrics to open locks, but doors that lead out of staff facilities and into guest areas open from the inside without requiring such biometrics.

**Lighting:** The resort has simulated day and night phases. Each lasts about 9 hours with 3 hours of twilight between each phase. A simulated sun in a lightly clouded sky shines through the sophisticated optics built into the ceiling during the day phase. Hidden panels produce a pleasant and warming "sunlight," providing bright light in "outside" areas. This light lacks any potentially harmful radiation, though in some areas, drones can provide low-level UV light for species that enjoy tanning. The manufactured lighting in indoor areas provides normal light. During the night phase, the windows show the resort's actual exterior, a spectacular starscape. These stars are gradually revealed when the simulated "sun" goes down and fade as it rises. During the night phase, panels on and within buildings provide dim light in most areas, some projecting holographic images of burning braziers. Guests can adjust indoor lighting to normal light when desired.

**Services:** New Elysium has fewer staff members than normal due to lower guest occupancy during the reopening event. Holograms, robots with virtual personalities, and simple drones perform numerous minor services, further reducing the need for personnel. Most areas rely on drones for menial tasks while traditional staff oversee constructs and interaction with guests. For instance, the Hollows Tavern (area **A8**) has living staff members who serve as bartender and host, while guests place their orders on consoles and are served by drones. A few drones are typical domestic models

(*Starfinder Armory* 101), while the rest are smaller, simpler units governed by New Elysium central computer servers that provide core functionality and personality.

Unless otherwise indicated, the resort offers staff-assisted service from 7 A.M. until 7 P.M., mid-dawn until mid-dusk. Most such features remain open at other hours but are automated. In addition, guests can have refreshments delivered from most eateries to anywhere else in the resort. Most amenities are free for event guests. Any gambling requires guests to exchange their own money for electronic markers that can be redeemed only when a guest checks out and are applied first to the guest's bill, if applicable. If something requires payment, New Elysium prefers electronic debit with established financial institutions to credsticks containing untraceable credits, as limiting the amount of physical currency on hand deters pirate attacks. Guests who want to use credsticks are encouraged to make a deposit with guest services (area **B8**) before or during a stay.

## A. MAIN FLOOR

The main floor of New Elysium houses most of the resort's entertainment amenities. As the Keys to Elysium program contains a map of this area, feel free to describe each of the rooms to the players so they can choose where to go and what amenities to enjoy. The map for this area is on page 13.

### A1. DOCK HALLWAY

This hall leads to docking arms that extend out from the asteroid and provide berths for numerous ships. Several of New Elysium security's Ringworks Sentinels dock close to the resort in order to facilitate evacuation in the event of an emergency.

### A2. GREEN FIELDS

As the resort's park, Green Fields mimics an outdoor area on a temperate planet. It has broad lawns punctuated with trees and shrubs. Green Fields sports a pool that resembles a natural pond as well as a stream. This stream starts in an artificial waterfall from the back of a cave called the Grotto (area **A2b**) at the park's southern end, flowing out of the pond and then under the path near the dock hallway. The water passes into the Boundless Sunroom (area **B1**) and then circulates through water filtration tanks in area **B13** back into the waterfall. Two stairways allow access to the top of the waterfall, facilitating access to the walking path behind the waterfall and the diving boards above it. The Grotto has a bar and two climbing walls at its opening, one to the north and a smaller one near the maintenance cave (area **A2a**); this cave contains items used by Vorilynn—with the gardening drones' help—to maintain the park.

### A3. LOOP

The Loop is a recreational walkway that encircles the main floor, offering easy access to the various shops and theaters. Many windows along the Loop show holographic images of strange and beautiful landscapes or, with a request to Keys to Elysium, actual views of the asteroid outside. Loop Runners (area **A3a**),

A. MAIN FLOOR
1 SQUARE = 10 FEET

A1

A2

A3

A14

A4a

A4

A13

A17

A3a

A17

A5

A12

A8

A15a

A8

A16

A6a

A10

A11

A6

A6b

A8

A8

A6d

A15b

A6c

A6b

A6c

A7b

A6b

A6c

A6d

A7

A7a

A6c

A7c

A6c

A6c

a shop just outside of Green Fields, is the official starting point of the Loop and offers guests access to light personal transport, such as bicycles, trikes, and skates. Guests can acquire either muscle-powered or self-propelled versions of these vehicles, depending on needs and preferences.

## A4. Contemplation

For those who need a quiet place to relax, Contemplation, a lounge that provides comfortable seating, serves no intoxicants stronger than coffee, and permits no inhalation of materials that give off secondhand vapors. Contemplation boasts many skylights and a terrace open to the Loop, overlooking the dome above the Boundless Sunroom. The terrace also sports a gravity chute (area **A4a**) that allows a guest to leap into the chute and drop harmlessly into the sunroom.

## A5. Wandering Market

This shop is named the Wandering Market because most of its wares can be purchased using a computer console and delivered to a guest's room. In addition to a sundries shop, the market contains a holographic fashion boutique with cleaning and tailoring services, a multicultural grocery that includes a mk 3 culinary synthesizer (*Armory* 129), and a high-end gift shop that contains small-scale 3-D printing facilities. Business

partners provide the onsite goods, while anything else is guaranteed to be delivered within 6 days.

## A6. Hall of Splendors

The Hall of Splendors offers several varieties of performances and entertainment. This includes a concert hall (area **A6a**), high-stakes gambling halls (area **A6b**), rooms for private parties (area **A6c**) available for public reservation, and a couple of theaters (area **A6d**) that show blockbuster trivids and other productions. Most shows are holographic recordings, but the resort also occasionally hosts live performers of various types.

## A7. Muses Meeting Rooms

To facilitate conferences, conventions, and other gatherings, New Elysium has several meeting rooms collectively called the Muses, including two ballrooms, Wave Walker (area **A7a**) and Emerald Song (area **A7b**). This area also includes the Grand Court (area **A7c**), a boardroom-style meeting area. Except for the Grand Court, these halls can be customized with temporary walls to form tailored spaces.

## A8. Painted Forest Playrooms

The Painted Forest Playrooms contain amusements ranging from holovid games and VR tanks to holo-slots and other gambling games.

## A9. Hollows Tavern

Located next to one of the Painted Forest Playrooms, and always open, Hollows Tavern provides a sit-down area and a wide array of drinks and snacks, as well as a cashier for Playroom markers. The nearby Moon Pool works like other Playroom fountains, only bigger.

## A10. Taste of Elysium

The resort's finest restaurant, Taste of Elysium opens at noon and closes again at midnight. It offers a variety of fine cuisine, and wine from across the galaxy. When the resort is filled to maximum capacity, reservations are usually required, and formal or semiformal attire is preferred. The restaurant also includes a bar and a party room, both more relaxed regarding dress and reservations. Taste of Elysium offers room service during its service hours but restaurant staff won't deliver anywhere else in the resort unless catering an event in the Muses.

## A11. Lyrakien Cabaret

A secondary concert venue offering light dinner theater, Lyrakien Cabaret is perfect for intimate variety performances, such as spoken word, stand-up comedy, and acoustic music. The cabaret is open from 7 P.M. until 2 A.M.

## A12. Absalom Bistro

A walk-in restaurant with a casual dress code, Absalom Bistro offers an eclectic mid-tier dining experience. The bistro prides itself on serving a variety of Pact Worlds mainstays with touches of interstellar food and drink.

## A13. WILD APPLES

Boisterous fun is what Wild Apples does best, with simpler fare but ample entertainment, including trivia nights, viewings of sporting events from elsewhere in the system, and performances by live musicians. Wild Apples also has a small dance floor and two mechanical riding beasts. This bar remains open until 2 A.M.

## A14. AZURE SKY

Some guests want to relax with a view of the stars, and Azure Sky fulfills that desire 24 hours a day, with drink service until 2 A.M. This bar has ample seating encircled by a viewing area. All walls are transparent and set to display the stars and the nearby asteroids of the Diaspora.

## A15. ELEVATORS

New Elysium has two banks of four elevators. The bank at area **A15a** goes between all three levels of the resort. The other bank (area **A15b**) allows guests to move only between the lodging floor and the main floor. Biometric scanners allow authorized staff members to access the utilities room (area **B13**).

## A16. SPIRAL STAIRS

Two spiral staircases connect all three floors. These stairways have locked doors preventing guests from descending into the facilities section.

## A17. HIDDEN STAIRS

Two staircases that descend to the lower floor are concealed from view within these halls.

## B. LOWER FLOOR

New Elysium's lower floor houses more amenities as well as staff facilities. Technicians offer personal assistance during service hours or by appointment, robots provide numerous services including massage, and drones perform menial tasks such as retrieving towels or robes. Some areas of this floor are detailed further in Part 3.

## B1. BOUNDLESS SUNROOM

The sun always shines in the Boundless Sunroom. The area is warm and has a pool with swimming and diving areas. In addition, the chamber has an artificial waterfall that flows from the stream in Green Fields. This room also features a smaller pool that can create artificial current to challenge swimmers but includes an offshoot that always remains out of the current that is ideal for resting or wading. Within this room, a drone can provide exposure to UV light or similar solar radiation for recreational purposes. In addition, a grav chute allows a guest to step inside and leap harmlessly from this room up to Contemplation's terrace.

## B2. CHANGING ROOMS

These rooms provide privacy for guests about to use this floor's various amenities, allowing them to change into a swimsuit or gym clothes in private.

## B3. BURNING GLADES

A set of sealable atmospheric chambers, Burning Glades can accommodate species that have unusual atmospheric needs and want to spend time outside an environment suit. A Burning Glades chamber can also be used as a sauna or steam bath for species that have no need for unusual atmospheres.

## B4. GYM

New Elysium's large gym provides the latest in fitness equipment. Connected to the main exercise area are rooms used as dance studios or dojos (areas **B4a**), each fitted with holographic training gear. Keys to Elysium provides guided fitness classes that take place here.

## B5. ICE FOUNTAINS

This area is the counterpart to the Boundless Sunroom, with a view of the stars and pools of water that can be lukewarm, filled with ice chunks, or even completely frozen over.

## B6. TITAN'S REST

Guests who come to Titan's Rest receive wellness services, such as personal grooming, massages, aromatherapy, body wraps, and mud packs. Titan's Rest also contains New Elysium's medical facilities, which offer everything from first aid to augmentation. The PCs can purchase most augmentations here and have them installed.

**Treasure:** Although numerous augmentations and devices are flash manufactured with 3-D printers here, Titan's Rest has a lot of potential treasure in storage. Along with 10 doses of sprayflesh, 20 medpatches, 10 diagnostic lozenges (*Armory* 101), two dermal staplers (*Armory* 100), three nanite hypopens (two black and one white; *Armory* 106), and a subdermal extractor (*Armory* 108). A PC trained in Medicine can acquire enough gear here to assemble five advanced medkits. The medical facility also holds many *serums of healing* (10 mk 1 and four mk 2) and nine tier 1 medicinals (three each of analgesics, antitoxins, and sedatives) and a tier 2 sedative. Dr. Lominn doesn't allow the PCs to take any of these supplies, especially after the resort has been quarantined (see page 22), but when the PCs return here later, they can easily acquire supplies.

## B7. REFLECTIONS

Similar to Titan's Rest, Reflections is a salon offering simpler spa services, as well as personal styling and grooming.

## B8. GUEST SERVICES

This area provides various services for guests, including business-related amenities, catering orders for events, travel scheduling, and similar conveniences.

SIGNAL OF SCREAMS

CAMPAIGN OUTLINE

THE DIASPORA STRAIN

PART 1: TWILIGHT IN ELYSIUM

PART 2: WAKING NIGHTMARES

PART 3: PARTING THE GLOOM

CORRUPTED BY SHADOWS

HORROR CAMPAIGNS

ALIEN ARCHIVES

CODEX OF WORLDS

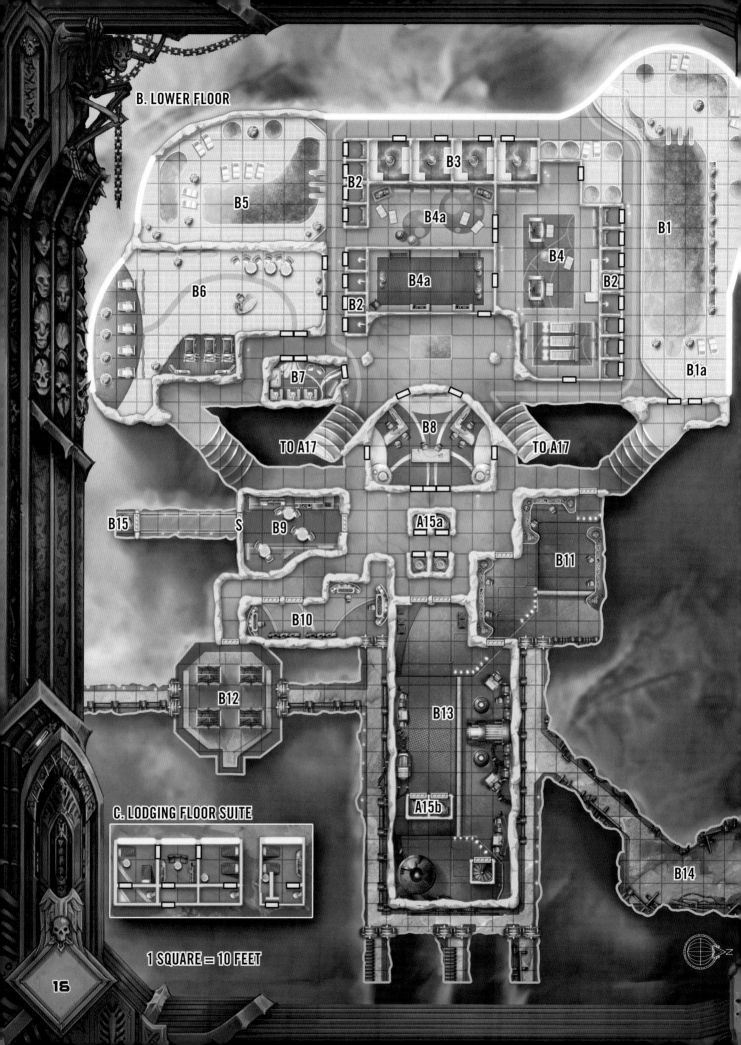

**B. LOWER FLOOR**

B5

B6

B2

B3

B4a

B4a

B2

B4

B4

B2

B1

B1a

B7

B8

TO A17

TO A17

B15

S

B9

A15a

B11

B10

B12

B13

A15b

B14

**C. LODGING FLOOR SUITE**

**1 SQUARE = 10 FEET**

## B9. Staff Lounge

A comfortable and isolated chamber, this lounge provides staff with a refuge from the wider resort during their breaks. A mk 3 culinary synthesizer (*Armory* 129) is built into the lounge's wall. A hidden door to the south (Perception DC 40) is locked with an exceptional lock (Engineering DC 40 to open).

After the PCs return from the mines at the end of Part 2, they encounter Dr. Lominn in this area during **Event 12**.

## B10. Security Center

This room—an administrative office and armory for security personnel—is closed to the public. Resort security handles several different duties in six four-person squads. Each squad rotates crewing of one of the resort's three Sentinel starships. Engineers and gunners have varied responsibilities, which can include facilities maintenance and patrol or guard details. Captains and pilots serve most shifts as security guards. Security specialists aren't expected to interact much with guests, although a few work as trainers in the gym.

**Treasure:** The security specialists keep their gear with them. However, the office contains a pair of lockers (each locked with biometric locks that require a successful DC 40 Engineering check to open) that contain three static arc rifles, 10 high-capacity batteries, two flash grenades II, five stickybomb grenades II, and 100 binders. The second locker contains a *mk 1 null-space chamber* along with any gifts the Buzzblades' gave to Kane Zaphol during **Event 3**.

## B11. Tech Workshop

The tech workshop contains drone recharging stations, work counters and tables, and tools. On the eastern wall is a large set of ventilation fans about 15 feet across, some of which turn slowly while others remain off. These fans are part of a cooling tunnel, a utility passage lined with pipes and automatic strips that illuminate to provide dim light. A rougher but similar tunnel branches off from there toward area **B14**.

The PCs find the remnants of a gloomwing attack here during **Event 8** and have an even creepier encounter here during **Event 11**.

**Treasure:** Most of the gear in this room is too bulky to carry away, but the workshop contains countless tools. The PCs can assemble numerous tool kits and two specialty tool kits (one armorsmithing kit and one weaponsmithing kit) from the equipment here.

## B12. Server Room

The four banks of servers in this squarish room operate all of the resort's technical aspects. The large fans to the north and south help keep the computers cool. New Elysium staff don't have much call to access this room when things are running well. The servers statistics and what they can be used to access are explained on page 37.

The PCs have a major altercation here with the corrupted members of the Buzzblades during **Event 13**.

## B13. Utilities Room

This enormous room houses several power cores that provide energy to the resort, as well as life support, water circulation and purification, and matter recycling facilities. Despite the cooling tunnels, vents, and numerous fans, it can get quite warm in here.

## B14. Mine Entrance

In the cooling tunnels, a branch leads to a junction room with myriad pipes going through the wall near a closed blast door. This area is detailed further in **Event 8**.

## B15. Deep Elevator

This elevator comes from the mines in Dr. Gragant's lab. If the PCs discover this area before Part 3, they find only the top of a deep shaft, with no obvious way of restoring power to the elevator.

# C. LODGING FLOOR

New Elysium has a third level above the main floor, where guest lodgings are located. Inside these rooms, opaque walls contain customizable windows and skylights similar to the viewing areas of New Elysium's public areas. Resort rooms feature many comforts, such as plush bedding, whirlpool baths, and private bars. The map on page 16 shows a typical suite and a typical double-occupancy room. Some variation exists, such as larger corner units and chambers with customizable atmosphere. Most resort amenities can be specially ordered from a guest's room, such as trivid theater presentations, vidscreen projections of live performances, fine food, and spa treatments.

This floor has several airlocks to allow for emergency evacuation. Biometric locks seal these airlocks but unlock if a staff-initiated computer override is sent from the server room.

# NPC INTERACTIONS

Nothing is scheduled to happen before the opening party (see **Event 3**). Ask the players how the PCs spend their time, and run a short scene, perhaps introducing an NPC or two (see Key Characters on page 6).

**Buzzblades:** If the PCs came to the *Goal Runner*'s aid, the Buzzblades—particularly Beryldor, Kofehsu, and Yazeloya—are friendly toward them. These Buzzblades ask the PCs to participate in activities with them, such as dinner, playing in the park, swimming, shows, and gambling. Lomer and Virlae are rowdier than their teammates and are ready to party, so they invite like-minded PCs to Wild Apples for heavy drinking and might even invite PCs back to their rooms. Zidhil keeps to himself, but will discuss the sport of brutaris with a fan.

If the PCs avoided helping the *Goal Runner*, the Buzzblades are indifferent toward them. Beryldor and Yazeloya are the most personable, cordially greeting the PCs in the halls and engaging in conversation when approached. Lomer and Virlae talk only to PCs who seem to share their boisterous attitudes. Kofehsu and Zidhil seldom interact with the PCs. If the team learns from the PCs that the party left *Goal Runner* to its fate (no other NPCs reveal this fact yet), the Buzzblades

SIGNAL OF SCREAMS

CAMPAIGN OUTLINE

THE DIASPORA STRAIN

PART 1: TWILIGHT IN ELYSIUM

PART 2: WAKING NIGHTMARES

PART 3: PARTING THE GLOOM

CORRUPTED BY SHADOWS

HORROR CAMPAIGNS

ALIEN ARCHIVES

CODEX OF WORLDS

become unfriendly, and Lomer, Virlae, and Yazeloya become particularly ill-disposed toward the PCs.

**Staff:** The PCs interact with staff by engaging in the resort's various amenities. The workers are friendly but endeavor to give the guests space. Among the named NPCs, Filip and Vorilynn are most accessible at this point, although you can introduce Dr. Lominn or Rhissona to a spa-goer or someone who gets injured during an athletic activity.

**Others:** Most guests interact with the PCs only in the casual way strangers sharing a recreational space might. The PCs might meet Romi and Indigo-13 in quieter venues on the resort, such as Contemplation. If any PC is renowned in a technical field, Romi might know her and strike up a conversation. Tok could approach well-known PCs to interview them or ask permission to film aspects of their stay. Cthesa seeks out PCs reputed to have traveled to unusual locales, especially those who have been to the Azlanti Star Empire. Other guest interactions are up to you.

## EVENT 2: QUESTIONING PIRATES

If the PCs disabled any Diasporan Raider (or if the New Elysium security staff was able to run one down), a few captured pirates are being held in one of the Sentinel's brigs. To remind players about these captives, Filip Kallsner might contact the PCs to inform them they have rights to the pirates' gear (assuming they helped defeat the pirates). If they want, the PCs can talk to the pirates on the day of the opening party. Filip says the pirates are scheduled for transfer into the Stewards' custody the next day.

Elysium security personnel escort the PCs onboard a Sentinel (see the map on the inside the back cover) to the brig, which has a barred, force-field augmented door that people can speak and see each other through. The two captive pirates are **Caenan** (NE female half-orc operative) and **Wenmar** (NE male korasha lashunta soldier), the pilot and gunner of one of the Diasporan Raiders, respectively. These ne'er-do-wells start with an attitude of hostile, insulting and laughing at the PCs while suggesting other pirates will soon avenge their capture, and jokingly asking for intoxicants. A PC who succeeds at a DC 34 Diplomacy check or DC 25 Intimidate check can alter the pirates' attitudes to unfriendly. Bringing the pirates alcohol automatically improves their attitude to unfriendly, but the PCs must first convince the indifferent security guards to allow this (with a successful DC 23 Bluff or Diplomacy check) or surreptitiously pass the liquor through the door's meal chute (with a successful DC 25 Sleight of Hand check).

If the PCs improve the pirates' attitudes to indifferent or better, the miscreants grow deadly serious. Caenan relates a tale about the asteroid New Elysium now occupies. Years ago, the place was an abandoned mine. Talk around the Diaspora suggested that some corporation built a facility within the old tunnels, but most believed the rumor was false or that such a place would have heavy security. Later "chinwag" said that people "got disappeared on this rock." A few bold pirates went

to "see what's what" over the years, but as no one who went in came out, most pirates avoided the place. Then, about 2 decades ago, something "right bad" happened inside the asteroid. A shirren pirate named Kizkota who visited the asteroid was able to transmit a message that warned others that the place "was turned inside out" and advised them to avoid it at all costs. Of course, pirates still traveled here anyway, and those who made it out talked about ghosts in machines, living shadows, and "mates" who disappeared in the tunnels.

Caenan finishes up by saying, "This place is full of hungry ghosts, mark me."

If asked, Filip can confirm the asteroid was a mine owned by Ulrikka Clanholdings. He dismisses the rest of the story as "pirate fantasy." After all, New Elysium has been on the asteroid for 5 years with no issues. A PC who succeeds at a DC 30 Computers check can locate a hobbyist conspiracy archive called Asteroid Anecdotes that confirms portions of the story with fewer details. However, the archive identifies the asteroid by its number, D-334H, which can be traced to Ulrikka—who abandoned it in 275 AG. With another successful DC 30 Computers check, a PC can uncover the fact that Eclipse Innovations registered ownership of the asteroid in 293 AG and sold it again 4 years later to a company called Vercara Holdings. Vercara held the asteroid until 311 AG, when Paradise Resorts bought it and began building New Elysium. A PC who succeeds at a DC 35 Computers check discovers that, through a few other companies, Eclipse indirectly owns Vercara Holdings.

**Treasure:** The PCs have salvage rights to the pirates' gear. Each pirate has defrex hide armor, a tactical dueling sword, a thunderstrike sonic pistol, a frag grenade II, and one battery. The pirate vessel had a corona artillery laser onboard, along with two high-capacity batteries. These items can be sold at most New Elysium shops for 10% of their value.

**Story Award:** Award the PCs 1,600 XP for learning the pirates' tale.

## EVENT 3: OPENING PARTY

As soon as everyone's ready, you can advance time to the opening party, which is at 6 P.M. on the day after the PCs docked at the resort. When the PCs arrive, read or paraphrase the following.

---

Three double doors open into a long hall decked out for a classy party. Opposite the doors is a stage raised from the main floor by several steps, where a holographic chamber orchestra with a dozen members plays softly. The floor before the stage is open. To the right and left sides of the room are dining tables near sideboards, each set with a lavish buffet, beverage fountains, and ice sculptures depicting sleek animals from various worlds. There is a bar next to each buffet. Well-dressed guests eat, drink, and mingle, and a few couples dance in the open space near the stage.

---

SIGNAL OF SCREAMS

CAMPAIGN OUTLINE

THE DIASPORA STRAIN

PART 1: TWILIGHT IN ELYSIUM

PART 2: WAKING NIGHTMARES

PART 3: PARTING THE GLOOM

CORRUPTED BY SHADOWS

HORROR CAMPAIGNS

ALIEN ARCHIVES

CODEX OF WORLDS

Most guests and staff are in attendance. Food and drink come from the Taste of Elysium restaurant (area **A10**), and after 30 minutes, drones begin to offer guests various bubbly drinks for an upcoming toast. At the 45-minute mark, the holographic orchestra fades, and Filip takes the stage with Dr. Lominn, both carrying their own refreshments.

---

Filip says, in an amplified voice, "Dear guests, as most of you know, my name is Filip Kallsner, and I'm your host here at New Elysium." He gestures toward his companion on the stage, saying, "This is Dr. Sidrani Lominn, who manages our spa and medical facilities. She's my counterpart in making sure everything's just right for you. Dr. Lominn?"

Raising her voice to address the guests, Dr. Lominn says, "We're happy to have all of you with us. We know you'll love your stay, and we hope you'll tell everyone you know just how much you enjoyed it. This celebration is just the beginning."

Filip and Dr. Lominn raise their glasses.

"Here's to a blissful stay in New Elysium," says Filip. "Please enjoy the rest of your evening!"

---

After the toast, Filip and Dr. Lominn leave the stage, and the holographic orchestra resumes. A few other events might occur during the party.

**Buzzblade Thanks:** Yazeloya and a few Buzzblades take the stage to publicly thank the PCs and New Elysium security (to the degree they deserve). If the PCs didn't help the *Goal Runner*, the team instead thanks New Elysium security and Kane Zaphol.

In either case, the team offers their rescuers season tickets to Buzzblades home games on Absalom Station. In addition, Zidhil gives the rescuers his *illuminating merciful wrack devastation blade*, used in 11 seasons and engraved with all the names of Buzzblades at the resort. The *illuminating* fusion creates purple and white light, the Buzzblades' team colors. Yazeloya presents the rescuers the suit of lashunta ringwear III she used in the most recent season, complete with jump jets in one upgrade slot. The other Buzzblades give the group a *called fusion seal* (7th) and a *merciful fusion seal* (7th), commonly used on brutaris weapons, as well as two *illuminating fusion seals* (7th) like the one on Zidhil's blade. The PCs have a chance to acquire this gear in the Security Center (area **B10**) later if Kane Zaphol received these presents.

**Other Interactions:** The PCs can interact with any of the key NPCs (see page 6). Dr. Lominn hovers near Filip and other resort staff, dancing with Kane Zaphol once or twice. It is easy to strike up a conversation with her. Unless the PCs engage her, Rhissona Avran acts the part of a wallflower, occasionally conversing with Vorilynn. Unless speaking with interested PCs, both leave early. Romi and Indigo-13 mingle and talk, although Indigo-13 takes Romi onto the dance floor during slower songs. Cthesa moves about the area, happily chatting with guests, including the PCs, and taking mental notes. Tok films the party, especially when Lomer and Virlae take to the dance floor during faster songs; the two athletes get more and more inebriated as the night wears on.

**Security Breaches:** If the PCs aided the *Goal Runner*, at some point in the night—when one or more PCs are in a conversation with Indigo-13, Romi, and Yazeloya—head of security Kane Zaphol walks up to the group and chides the PCs for "interfering in a New Elysium security issue." If the PCs don't stand up for themselves, Yazeloya tells Kane off on their behalf. Indigo-13 starts to back her up, but Romi interjects graciously, suggesting the PCs did what they thought was right and no one can fault them for that. Kane then leaves the group alone.

If the PCs didn't come to the *Goal Runner*'s assistance, while the PCs are mingling with the Buzzblades, Kane Zaphol walks over and comments that the PCs were lucky not to have been caught up in the pirate skirmish, since they were nearby during the incident. The Buzzblades react poorly to this information, questioning the PCs about their ship and why they didn't help. From this point on, the Buzzblades are unfriendly toward the PCs, and Yazeloya considers them to be cowards. A PC who succeeds at a DC 25 Sense Motive check can see the reaction pleases Kane. If confronted, he denies his intentions and silently decides that the astute PC is a potential problem.

Filip apologizes on Kane's behalf if the PCs report his behavior. Filip later scolds Kane, earning the PCs his ire during **Event 15**.

**Shadow Sighting:** As the PCs leave the party, the character with the highest Perception bonus notices—out of the corner of an eye—a bizarre, vaguely humanoid-shaped shadow moving in the hallway against the light. The phenomenon is gone when the PCs look more closely. Teodhor was watching nearby and used his *shadow body* spell to disappear.

# EVENT 4: THE SEEDS OF CORRUPTION

Over the next 7 days, the PCs can relax however they like. Similar to the first day, ask what they'd like to do, using the resorts amenities as a guide. Soon though, they will begin to experience the corrupting influence of Dr. Gragant's shadow signal.

## CONTRACTING SHADOW CORRUPTION

Starting 2 days after the opening party, at the end of the day before resting for 8 hours, each PC must attempt a Will saving throw (DC = 10 + half the PC's level + any increase from the Keys to Elysium curse [see page 10] + 1 for each previous save attempted). This DC increases by 1 if the PC has engaged in any malicious activity that day, such as purposefully deceiving others or harming innocents (including those in the throes of phantasms—see **Event 5**). Such a PC might remember the triggering activity with misplaced emotion, such as righteous anger after harming someone, or deep pleasure for stealing. You should roll these saving throws in secret.

Each PC who fails this save gains the dormant shadow corruption (see page 42) and experiences disturbing thoughts or dreams during the rest cycle. From that point until the end of the Adventure Path, a PC afflicted with shadow corruption must attempt another Will saving throw at the end of each day before resting for 8 hours, gaining a shadow corruption manifestation on each failure. A PC can spend a Resolve Point to ignore a failed save and avoid gaining a manifestation. If you like, you can also roll these saving throws in secret, but give the PC the option to spend a Resolve Point if she fails by asking if she wants to give in to the almost inaudible whispers in her mind that promise power and pleasure. If she consents to the suggestion, she can choose which manifestation she gains.

To speed up play, you can assume that when days pass in which nothing much happens (such as an uneventful starship journey through the Drift) the PCs either succeed at their saving throws or spend the necessary Resolve Points to avoid gaining manifestations. Of course, a player might decide his character is always tempted by the corruption and might want to make those decisions on a day-to-day basis, but remember to warn such a player that a PC who gains more than four manifestations essentially becomes an evil NPC under your control.

NPCs are affected as the story requires rather than according to these mechanics. Many of them, such as resort staff, have been exposed to the influence for a longer time. Others, such as the neutral and evil members of the staff and Buzzblades, are more susceptible.

## PHANTASMS

During this adventure, it's important the players begin to doubt what their characters sense and know. To aid with that, this adventure introduces phantasms, a delusion with comprehensive sensory aspects experienced only by those subjected to them. Phantasms aren't real, but the victims believe them to be real for the duration of the effect. The phantasms in this adventure are extensions of Dr. Gragant's influence on the asteroid and increase the PCs susceptibility to the corruption of the shadow signal.

When describing a phantasm, do so in stages, starting with just enough information to provoke a response. Allow the player to attempt actions. Then have the phantasm react to those actions, going back and forth between character and phantasm until the phantasm ends. While a phantasm lasts, describe it as if it's real, including aspects such as conditions and damage. As all phantasms are similar in that they affect a PC's mind, they're impossible to escape while they last. See Sample Phantasms on page 22 for examples.

A phantasm functions like a combination of a curse and a trap. When using the phantasm stat block, keep the following in mind.

**Targets:** A specific phantasm might affect only one target or several targets at once. The phantasm affects each target separately, so each target must end the effect for itself. Even if all affected PCs succeed at the initial save against a phantasm, the group still receives XP from the phantasm.

**Saving Throws:** As they are similar to illusions, phantasms require their victims to attempt Will saving throws. However, to reinforce the illusion, write down all the PCs' saving throw modifiers ahead of time and ask them to attempt different saves based on each phantasm's nature. Then, secretly add a PC's Will save modifier to that PC's die result. Phantasms are mind-affecting effects, so don't forget any modifiers that apply to such effects. Open rolls with unreliable results reinforce the "reality" of phantasms in the minds of players more than secret rolls.

Even if a PC succeeds at the Will save, a phantasm causes a brief hallucination related to its full content before ending. The phantasm imposes its full effect on any PC who fails his saving throw. This effect is like a waking dream, so it can seem to last longer than it actually does.

Those unaffected by a phantasm can try to help victims break out of the illusion. Doing so is difficult because the victim sees everyone else in terms dictated by the phantasm. A character who succeeds at a Bluff, Diplomacy, or Intimidate check (DC = 15 + 1-1/2 × the CR of the phantasm) allows one affected person to attempt a new saving throw against the phantasm with a +4 circumstance bonus. A character can grant this saving throw and bonus for one additional affected person for every 5 the result of her check exceeds the DC.

**Combat:** The initiative, AC, saving throw bonuses, and attack statistics for a phantasm exist to aid your description. A phantasm can't be defeated in combat. Instead, it lasts until its duration elapses or the victim meets the ending conditions. Though the damage dealt by a phantasm reduces a target's Stamina Points, it can never reduce a target's Hit Points, and you shouldn't tell the players that right away. When a phantasm ends, any Hit Points a target seemed to have lost immediately return. If a character believes she has been reduced to 0 Hit Points by a phantasm, she instead falls unconscious for 1d4 rounds (ending the phantasm for her).

While any HP damage dealt by phantasm is illusory, someone in the throes of one can deal or take real damage. For instance, if a victim affected by a phantasm attacks a monstrous figure that is actually another person, that person can be hurt. A victim who steps into boiling water takes damage from that water. However, anything that harms a victim during a phantasm that isn't part of the phantasm (such as being punched in the face by another character) allows the victim to attempt another saving throw just after the harmful effect occurs. If the result of an affected victim's action would deal damage to the victim (such as grabbing a knife by the wrong end), this additional saving throw can be attempted before the victim takes damage instead of after.

**Conclusion:** When a phantasm ends, any Stamina Point damage the phantasm dealt remains, and the victim is shaken for 1 minute. No other effects from the phantasm linger.

## SHIP SIGNOFF

During this week, one minor mundane issue intrudes on the PCs' relaxation (and possible corruption). Filip asks the PCs to sign off on the repairs and requested modifications to their starship (all taken care of by Paradise Resorts). He looks slightly haggard and seems less chipper during this meeting, but waves off any concern the PCs might express with a cheerful laugh and a sardonic "a devil's work is never done!"

**Customization:** A phantasm has statistics like a trap (see Table 11–14: Trap Statistics on page 412 of the *Core Rulebook*), and it typically has a CR equal to half the level of the PCs' APL (rounded down). A phantasm has only one AC (the highest for its CR), all good saves, and a +4 bonus to combat maneuvers. A phantasm deals the full amount of damage listed in the table (of an appropriate type) with a successful attack, or half this amount of damage if it always hits. You can add other rules to facilitate the delusion, such as monster special abilities.

Use the main statistics below for phantasms in this adventure, though their exact effects differ from phantasm to phantasm (see Sample Phantasms on page 22).

## PHANTASM CR 3

**XP 800**

**Type** curse (mind-affecting); **Save** Will DC 14 (17 if in possession of a comm unit cursed by Keys to Elysium [see page 10])

**Trigger** location; **Init** +8; **Duration** 10 rounds; **Reset** none

**AC** 17; **Fort** +6; **Ref** +6; **Will** +6

**Attack** +13 (+17 for combat maneuvers) or automatic (6d6 or 3d6 if automatic)

**Effect** depends on the results of the initial save and the specifics of the phantasm (see above)

## TEODHOR SIGHTINGS

During a phantasm, a PC might see Teodhor from a distance, mistaking him for part of the phantasm. Later, the PCs might hear about a guest seeing a flayed halfling or child. Teodhor moves quickly and stealthily, using his abilities to avoid being pinned down. Anyone who gets close enough to Teodhor might be affected by his unnerving gaze (see page 60), but that unpleasantness should seem like part of a phantasm. Avoid allowing the PCs to confront the velstrac until they reach area **H**.

## EVENT 5: PHANTASM ENCOUNTERS

Starting on the morning on the fourth day and continuing through the end of the tenth day, the PCs should face at least a dozen phantasms. Switch up which PC experiences a phantasm each day, but multiple PCs should be involved in a few phantasms together, sowing more doubt about what is real and what isn't. Sometime during this period, at least one PC should witness another guest or PC in the throes of a phantasm, giving the onlooker an attempt to shake the other character out of the fugue. Remind your players the other guests are normal (if famous) people, not villains or monsters.

The most effective phantasms are personal. You can use the examples below as written or as inspiration to create your own phantasms that are most likely to provoke a response from the PCs experiencing them. Many of these examples are also appropriate for multiple PCs to experience simultaneously.

**Story Award:** Grant the PCs 800 XP for each phantasm they face, whether the PCs succeed at the initial saving throw against it or not.

## Sample Phantasms

You can use the following phantasms or create your own for use in this adventure.

**Appeal to Vice:** The PC catches a glimpse of an attractive companion beckoning him to step into a private chamber. If the PC fails the saving throw against this phantasm, he is compelled to enter the room. He believes he is engaging intimately with the companion for the duration of the phantasm until the companion's face and body transforms suddenly into a disgusting, rotting corpse (or something equally horrid) before disappearing completely. This phantasm deals no damage.

**Creepy Peepers:** While the PC grooms himself, he feels something in his throat. If he looks in a mirror, he sees his mouth is filled with a monstrous eye, while his normal eyes are gone. If he succeeds at the initial saving throw, this vision fades. Otherwise, he begins to suffocate (taking 3d6 bludgeoning damage each round) as the mirror cracks. Trying to take any action is futile, as his appendages become limp and weak. The phantasm slowly ends as the crack reverses itself in slow motion, until the PC can breathe again.

**Cruel Consumable:** While the PC is partaking of a meal, this phantasm tricks her into believing something inedible (like a plate or glass) is part of the food (such as a piece of bread or candy). If she fails the initial saving throw, she mistakenly bites down on the object, which deals 3d6 piercing or slashing damage unless she succeeds at a second saving throw to notice the mistake in time.

**Doppelganger:** As the PC talks to an NPC, she sees that NPC pass nearby. If she succeeds at the initial saving throw, the NPC she was talking to has vanished when she turns back. Otherwise, the NPC double suddenly attacks, continuing to do so for the remainder of the phantasm, dealing 6d6 bludgeoning damage with each successful strike. At the end of the phantasm, the hostile NPC disappears.

**Evil Signs:** The PC begins to see signs of evil everywhere—blood runs down the walls, nearby NPCs' eyes turn white, a vidscreen shows eldritch symbols, and so on. If she fails the initial saving throw, these visions persist for the remainder of the phantasm, and any voices she hears sound like the terrifying grunts of fiends. She also believes that any attempts to help her are actually threatening motions. When the phantasm ends, so do the signs of evil.

**Infection Scare:** Upon scratching an itch, the PC notices a strange lesion on his skin. If he succeeds at the initial saving throw, the wound fades away. Otherwise, he feels compelled to continue to dig at the lesion, dealing 3d6 slashing damage to himself each round as he uncovers increasingly worse signs of disease under the skin. When the phantasm ends, the "infected" area is merely red from constant rubbing.

**Intemperate Jealousy:** A wave of fierce envy toward a fellow guest overcomes the PC. It passes quickly if she succeeds at the initial save. Otherwise, she is compelled to voice her emotions in the loudest possible terms for the remainder of the phantasm, which could lead to a physical altercation. Afterward, she can barely remember what aroused her ire.

**Monster Sighting:** The PC mistakes a fellow guest or staff member for a horrendous monster. If he succeeds at the initial saving throw, he quickly realizes he was mistaken, but otherwise he is compelled to attack the fellow guest or staff member as if it were that monster for the remainder of the phantasm. The monster appears to fight back, dealing 6d6 slashing or piercing damage on each successful strike. This phantasm is best used when a second PC is nearby to stop the first from killing an innocent person.

**Personal Injury:** During an otherwise simple activity, such as exercising or eating dinner, the PC clumsily injures herself. If she succeeds at the initial saving throw, the injury amounts to nothing. Otherwise, she begins to take 3d6 bleed damage each round for the remainder of the phantasm. Worse yet, any of her attempts to stop the bleeding only make it worse, and those around her seem ignorant of the gouts of blood spraying all over. When the phantasm ends, the wound has disappeared.

**Sensory Failure:** A PC with telepathy is suddenly overcome by piercing telepathic noise. If he fails the initial saving throw, his mind is overwhelmed, "shutting down" all of his senses for the remainder of the phantasm. If he is alone when this occurs, he could stumble into danger. Either way, as the phantasm wanes, the PC begins to sense a malevolent presence, as if someone were lightly tracing fingers across his skin.

**Service Mishap:** This phantasm occurs to a PC when he is attempting to relax in a hot tub alone. If he succeeds at the initial saving throw, he realizes he has set the temperature of the water far too high, but he has no memory of doing so. Otherwise, he steps unknowingly into the boiling water, taking 6d6 fire damage unless he succeeds at an additional saving throw. By all accounts, the mishap wasn't caused by technological malfunction, but rather a seemingly deliberate act by the PC.

**Space Danger:** The PC hears a soft pop and hiss. Looking around, she notices a spreading crack in a nearby window. If she succeeds at the initial save, the crack is just a trick of the light. Otherwise, the spreading damage eventually causes a small breach, and (with a successful combat maneuver) the resulting loss of pressure drags her 10 feet closer each round. The PC's legs give out, rendering her immobile. If pulled against the broken window, she is grappled and takes 3d6 bludgeoning damage at the end of each turn until she escapes or the phantasm ends.

**Wounded Creature:** The PC hears a faint scratching coming from a nearby ventilation duct. If she fails the initial saving throw, she sees a rodent with obvious signs of poisoning limp into view. However, her muscles freeze up and she can only watch as the creature dies slowly and painfully, and then quickly rots away into nothingness. The phantasm deals no damage.

## ESCALATING TENSIONS

As the PCs, guests, and staff experience phantasms, people begin lashing out at one another, especially those—such as the Buzzblades or security personnel—who were already in positions of strength. Over these days, evidence of minor injuries, some clearly self-inflicted, can be spotted on various NPCs. Others show signs of corruption manifestations such as weight loss, paleness, darkening eyes, poor demeanor, lethargy, and apathy.

If the PCs harm others during a phantasm, security personnel might have to step in. If a PC is injured, security takes her to Dr. Lominn for medical evaluation. As the days wear on, Dr. Lominn receives more and more cases related to the phantasms. She begins to suspect that a strange contagion could be sweeping through the resort, and might reveal that fact to inquisitive PCs. The doctor has no evidence to back up this theory, since most people appear to be physically fine during exams and subsequent tests. See **Event 6** for more about interacting with Dr. Lominn during this period.

Rumors also start to spread about a disease or contamination of the food or water. An NPC mentions or is overheard saying that staff members are missing or sick. More guests start carrying weapons, mostly small arms. Cthesa looks unwell on the seventh day, claiming poor sleep. She can't be found on the eighth day if anyone looks for her, and Tok asks if anyone has seen her on the morning of the ninth day. Cthesa's fate is ultimately revealed during **Event 8**.

## EVENT 6: SOFT QUARANTINE (CR 7)

On the seventh day, or as soon as the PCs attempt to leave the resort, security adds a constant guard rotation near the dock hallway (area **A1**) outside of Green Fields (area **A2**). Within the docking area, the airlocks to docked vessels can't be opened without a security override.

**Creatures:** If the PCs question the two security specialists on duty, they report only that they're stationed here on Dr. Lominn's orders. The guards refuse to let anyone past and won't divulge the security override code to open the airlocks. They're all too happy to see a little action if someone provokes them; PCs who do so face detainment. The security specialists take any PCs who attack to a Ringworks Sentinel brig, and Dr. Lominn releases them a few hours later.

### NEW ELYSIUM SECURITY SPECIALISTS (2)    CR 5

**XP 1,600 each**
Male and female human soldier
LN Medium humanoid (human)
**Init** +5; **Senses** darkvision 60 ft.;
**Perception** +11

**DEFENSE**                                          **HP** 70 each
**EAC** 17; **KAC** 20
**Fort** +7; **Ref** +5; **Will** +6
**Defensive Abilities** guard's protection

**OFFENSE**
**Speed** 30 ft.
**Melee** tactical baton +11 (1d4+8 B)
**Ranged** static arc pistol +14 (1d6+5 E; critical arc 2) or
flash grenade I +14 (explode [5 ft., blinded 1d4 rounds, DC 15]) or
stickybomb grenade II +14 (explode [15 ft., entangled 2d4 rounds, DC 15])
**Offensive Abilities** fighting styles (guard)

**STATISTICS**
**Str** +3; **Dex** +5; **Con** +2; **Int** +0; **Wis** +1; **Cha** +0
**Skills** Athletics +11, Intimidate +16, Piloting +11, Sense Motive +11
**Languages** Common
**Other Abilities** armor training
**Gear** estex suit III (infrared sensors), static arc pistol with 2 batteries (20 charges each), tactical baton, flash grenade I, stickybomb grenade II, binders, flashlight

**NEW ELYSIUM SECURITY SPECIALIST**

**Development:** If the PCs meet Dr. Lominn in the brig or because they want to ask her about the quarantine, she looks exhausted. However,

SIGNAL OF SCREAMS

CAMPAIGN OUTLINE

THE DIASPORA STRAIN

PART 1: TWILIGHT IN ELYSIUM

PART 2: WAKING NIGHTMARES

PART 3: PARTING THE GLOOM

CORRUPTED BY SHADOWS

HORROR CAMPAIGNS

ALIEN ARCHIVES

CODEX OF WORLDS

she's also honest with them. Stewards protocol calls for a soft quarantine in response to problems like those in New Elysium, and Dr. Lominn has implemented one and notified the Stewards. However, she has no idea what is causing the illnesses. The Stewards expect reports on ongoing quarantines and don't usually send their own investigators for fear of infection. A PC who succeeds at a DC 20 Sense Motive check determines not only that she's earnest, but also that she's worried. If the PCs can improve her indifferent attitude to friendly (Diplomacy DC 22) and ask her what's wrong, she reveals that Filip is faring poorly. He appears to be suffering from mental and physical exhaustion as well as depression; he's receiving care in his quarters.

Dr. Lominn comes to them eventually, especially if the PCs have handled the phantasms well. She asks for their assistance in keeping the other guests calm. This point is another opportunity for the PCs to talk to her and learn about the soft quarantine and Filip's illness.

**Story Award:** If the PCs interact peacefully with the New Elysium security specialists and learn more from Dr. Lominn about the soft quarantine, award them 3,200 XP, as if they had defeated the security specialists in combat.

## EVENT 7: BUZZBLADE ALTERCATION (CR 7)

As the PCs attempt to relax in a public area on the morning of the tenth day, perhaps in the Boundless Sunroom (area **B1**), Virlae acts as if one of them insulted her. Consider running this encounter with everyone unarmed and unarmored. If you do so, the two Buzzblades have an AC of 15 and use unarmed attacks. They might grab pieces of furniture or other objects to use as weapons.

**Creatures:** Virlae goes berserk and attacks the PCs. Lomer, who's nearby but not entirely aware of what's going on, joins the fight at her side. Other guests back off, but not Tok. He films the quarrel and eggs it on, making it more difficult to quell. Tok shuts up only if convinced (Diplomacy DC 21) or threatened (Intimidate DC 21) by a PC. A PC who succeeds at a DC 20 Sense Motive check can tell that Virlae is not acting rationally and that Lomer is only backing her up.

The PCs can calm the situation with a few well-placed words instead of fighting. Calming Virlae requires a successful DC 32 Diplomacy check made as a full action; this check takes a –5 penalty if any PC has attacked either of the Buzzblades that round. This check automatically fails if Tok is still in the room and meddling, but Lomer also backs down if Virlae does. If this Diplomacy check was successful, but Tok then thwarted the PCs' efforts, a PC can attempt another Diplomacy check (after shutting Tok up) in a future round with +5 circumstance bonus. Alternatively, a PC can convince Lomer not to fight with a successful DC 27 Diplomacy check made as a full action; the same constraints mentioned above apply to this check.

If the fight begins with unarmed and unarmored combatants and a PC grabs a weapon or begins dealing lethal damage with a spell or another ability, the Virlae grabs her own nearby weapon.

## LOMER                                            CR 5
**XP 1,600**
Agender android solarian
LE Medium humanoid (android)
**Init** +5; **Senses** darkvision 60 ft., low-light vision;
   Perception +11

### DEFENSE                                         HP 70
**EAC** 17; **KAC** 19
**Fort** +7; **Ref** +5; **Will** +6; +2 vs. disease, mind-affecting
   effects, poison, and sleep

### OFFENSE
**Speed** 30 ft.
**Melee** solar weapon +14 (1d6+7 B)
**Offensive Abilities** stellar revelations (black hole [25-ft.
   radius, pull 15 ft., DC 13], dark matter [DR 1/—], stellar rush
   [2d6 F, DC 13], supernova [10-ft. radius, 6d6 F, DC 13])

### TACTICS
**During Combat** Lomer sticks close to Virlae and manifests
   their solar weapon, a flat club. They make nonlethal
   attacks with their solar weapon (taking a –4 penalty to
   each), but they don't use their stellar revelations unless
   the situation becomes dire.
**Morale** Lomer backs down when reduced to fewer than
   40 Hit Points, but only if Virlae has also backed down.

### STATISTICS
**Str** +2; **Dex** +5; **Con** +0; **Int** +3; **Wis** +0; **Cha** +0
**Skills** Acrobatics +16, Athletics +11, Mysticism +11, Stealth +11
**Languages** Akitonian, Common
**Other Abilities** constructed, flat affect, solar manifestation
   (solar weapon), stellar alignment, upgrade slot
   (radiation buffer)
**Gear** d-suit I

## VIRLAE NILUFEH                                   CR 5
**XP 1,600**
Female korasha lashunta operative
LE Medium humanoid (lashunta)
**Init** +6; **Perception** +12

### DEFENSE                                         HP 65
**EAC** 17; **KAC** 18
**Fort** +4; **Ref** +7; **Will** +8
**Defensive Abilities** evasion

### OFFENSE
**Speed** 40 ft., climb 30 ft., swim 30 ft.
**Melee** merciful tactical switchblade +12 (1d4+8 S
   nonlethal) or
   unarmed strike (1d6+8 B nonlethal)
**Offensive Abilities** debilitating trick, trick attack +3d8
**Lashunta Spell-Like Abilities** (CL 5th)
   1/day—detect thoughts (DC 15)
   At will—daze (DC 15), psychokinetic hand

### TACTICS
**During Combat** Virlae doesn't pull any punches and
   attempts to use trick attack every round.

**Morale** Virlae finally backs down when reduced to fewer than 30 Hit Points.

## STATISTICS
**Str** +3; **Dex** +5; **Con** +2; **Int** +0; **Wis** +0; **Cha** +0
**Skills** Acrobatics +22, Athletics +22 (+30 to climb and swim), Bluff +12, Culture +12, Intimidate +17, Stealth +12
**Feats** Improved Unarmed Strike
**Languages** Castrovelian, Common; limited telepathy 30 ft.
**Other Abilities** operative exploits (uncanny mobility, versatile movement), specialization (daredevil)
**Gear** d-suit I, *merciful tactical switchblade*[AR]

**Development:** As the Buzzblades back down, hopefully before anyone can be seriously injured, two New Elysium security specialists (see page 23) show up and ask everyone to stand down. They take statements from everyone present, and it becomes clear that Virlae reacted to something that didn't actually happen. She doesn't apologize, but she admits that she doesn't feel well and agrees to see Dr. Lominn.

**Story Award:** If the PCs calm Virlae before she becomes too violent, award them XP as if they had defeated the two Buzzblades in combat.

## EVENT 8: CTHESA'S FATE (CR 8)
On the morning of the eleventh day, Dr. Lominn requests the PCs meet her in the Boundless Sunroom (area **B1**) and mentions they should be prepared to do some "dangerous work." The haggard-looking doctor takes them through the doors to the east and down the stairs toward the elevator banks (area **A15a**). There, a group of four security specialists (see page 23) are gathered, as well as Indigo-13, Rhissona Avran (who looks quite healthy), Romi, and Vorilynn.

Dr. Lominn discloses security has slain a "giant moth" that Romi spotted entering a ventilation duct near these elevators. The vent cover here is broken, and a PC who succeeds at a DC 25 Perception check notices a strange, silvery powder around the vent. A PC who succeeds at a DC 20 Perception check also notices the guards are tired, and while all are banged up, one was bitten through his armor and another suffered electrical burns that, if anyone asks, are from friendly fire; a PC who succeeds at a DC 20 Sense Motive check can see that the officer responsible for the friendly fire seems amused by it. Dr. Lominn and Rhissona treat the guards' wounds, and the doctor asks the

PCs and Vorilynn to check out the moth in area **B11**. Romi follows out of curiosity with an approving nod from Indigo-13.

Near the cooling fans is the corpse of an 8-foot-long moth with eerie shifting patterns on its wings. The moth's wounds, and a smell like burnt hair and ozone, are obvious. A PC who succeeds at a DC 20 Medicine check can tell the moth died from electrical shocks such as those generated by shock weapons. A PC who succeeds at a DC 21 Mysticism check identifies the creature as a gloomwing (see page 56; Vorilynn reveals this if the PCs don't succeed at this check). A pertinent fact about this outsider is that it lays eggs in prey that it has slain, and those eggs produce tenebrous worms (see page 59). A PC who examines the moth and succeeds at a DC 25 Medicine or Mysticism check can tell that it has recently laid several eggs. Vorilynn can again provide this information if needed.

A PC who succeeds at a DC 25 Perception check spots more dust, like that seen earlier around the vent, on the fan in the eastern wall. More powder inside the stone tunnel behind the fan suggests the gloomwing came from that area. Romi finds this residue if PCs miss it.

If the PCs report to Dr. Lominn before investigating further, she wonders whether these creatures have something to do with the strangeness occurring at the resort. She asks the PCs to go into the tunnels and look for more evidence while she has security clean up the mess and check the other cooling tunnels. On behalf of Paradise Resorts, she offers to pay the PCs 1,000 credits apiece for helping her contain this situation quickly and discretely. She'll increase her offer to 1,500 apiece if a PC succeeds at a DC 30 Diplomacy check; the PCs could gain circumstance bonuses to these negotiations based on how helpful they've been in other situations. If pressed as to why security can't completely handle the problem, the doctor reveals that a significant portion of the security team is unwell and resting in their quarters. If asked about the stone tunnels, Dr. Lominn reveals they were part of a mine that occupied the asteroid before the resort was built.

A successful DC 20 Engineering check is required to shut down the slow ventilation fans so the PCs can duck past them into the tunnel. Romi can aid on this check if need be. Neither the androids nor Vorilynn accompany the party into the tunnel. Automatic light strips in the tunnel provide dim light. Following the gloomwing's residue trail

VIRLAE NILUFEH

SIGNAL OF SCREAMS

CAMPAIGN OUTLINE

THE DIASPORA STRAIN

PART 1: TWILIGHT IN ELYSIUM

PART 2: WAKING NIGHTMARES

PART 3: PARTING THE GLOOM

CORRUPTED BY SHADOWS

HORROR CAMPAIGNS

ALIEN ARCHIVES

CODEX OF WORLDS

requires a successful DC 16 Survival check. If a PC succeeds by 10 or more, she also finds a few blood spatters along the ground. The trail leads down the northern tunnel, where the PCs can smell the faint scent of decay. The odor gets stronger as the PCs move down the tunnel, eventually reaching area **B14**. In the center of that chamber, they easily spot the distended corpse of Cthesa.

**Creatures:** A second gloomwing hides in the dim light on the ceiling near the blast door that leads deeper into the mines. It waits to attack until it is discovered or the PCs examine Cthesa's body. During the second round of combat with the gloomwing, or as soon as something disturbs Cthesa's corpse, three tenebrous worm hatchlings erupt from the body and attack. These worms are similar to those presented on page 59 but have yet to form their bristles.

## GLOOMWING                                          CR 4
**XP 1,200**

**HP** 50 (see page 56)

**TACTICS**

**During Combat** The gloomwing isn't hungry, but it is cornered and agitated. It attacks the creature that hurt it most or harmed the worms last round.

**Morale** The gloomwing has nowhere to flee, so it fights to the death.

## TENEBROUS WORM HATCHLINGS (3)          CR 4
**XP 1,200 each**

N Small outsider (extraplanar)

**Init** +3; **Senses** darkvision 60 ft.; **Perception** +10

**DEFENSE**                                        **HP** 50 each
**EAC** 16; **KAC** 18

**Fort** +6; **Ref** +6; **Will** +5

**Immunities** acid

**OFFENSE**
**Speed** 20 ft.

**Melee** bite +10 (1d4+5 P plus shadow acid; critical corrode 1d4)

**TACTICS**

**During Combat** The hungry hatchlings prefer to attack already wounded targets.

**Morale** Ravenous, the hatchlings fight to the death.

**STATISTICS**
**Str** +1; **Dex** +3; **Con** +5; **Int** −4; **Wis** +0; **Cha** −2

**Skills** Stealth +10

**SPECIAL ABILITIES**
**Shadow Acid (Su)** See page 59. This acid deals 2d4 acid damage in dim light, 1d4 acid damage in normal light, and 1 acid damage in bright light or darkness.

**Development:** The blast door to the north is locked (Engineering DC 35 to unlock; only Teodhor's biometrics can bypass the lock). A warning sign on the door notes that access to the mining tunnels on the other side is restricted.

Dr. Lominn doesn't have the authority to open the door and asks that it remain closed.

Dr. Lominn has a security robot collect Cthesa's remains and quietly bring them to area **B6**. If the PCs do so instead, she gives them each an extra 250 credits. Rhissona seems quite upset when she sees Cthesa's body, but she is only acting; a PC who succeeds at a Sense Motive check opposed by her Bluff check (she has a total skill bonus of +18) can tell something isn't quite right. If confronted, Rhissona feigns ignorance, claiming that she was fond of the travel writer's work.

Dr. Lominn doesn't ask the PCs to investigate Cthesa's death, but neither does she do anything to stop them. Investigating the shirren's quarters reveals nothing unusual. A PC who succeeds at a DC 25 Diplomacy check convinces the security team to allow the PCs to check vid footage of the past several nights. Alternatively, a PC can hack into the security feeds from any of the computer terminals found throughout the resort with a successful DC 28 Computers check. The footage shows Cthesa wandering the resort late on the seventh night, almost in a trance. She ends up in the Boundless Sunroom, and the eastern door opens on its own. She steps through it, reaching out as if greeting a friend or loved one. A PC who succeeds at a DC 27 Perception check while examining the footage notices a humanoid shadow moving against the light in a few different frames. If a PC casts *grave words* or *speak with dead* on Cthesa's corpse, it speaks feverishly about "following my brother" and the "flapping of dusty wings" before trailing off into incoherence.

Cthesa grew up on Verces and was involved in a horrible vehicle crash in the city of Nabokon when she was young, in which her younger brother and father were killed. A PC can attempt a DC 30 Culture check to recall this information or discover it on the infosphere with a successful DC 25 Computers check and a few hours of research.

**Treasure:** In addition to any pay they earned, the PCs can harvest the chitin from the gloomwings (see page 56).

**Story Award:** In addition to the XP they earn from the fight, if the PCs learn about what happened to Cthesa the night she disappeared, they earn 1,600 XP.

## PART 2: WAKING NIGHTMARES

The death of one of the guests and the appearance of strange creatures in the infrastructure of the resort are really only the beginning of the PCs' problems. The corruption of Dr. Gragant's shadow signal begins to swallow more and more of the guests, and the PCs will have to deal with the consequences.

## EVENT 9: HARD QUARANTINE (CR 9)
On the evening of the eleventh day, Dr. Lominn completely quarantines the resort, announcing over the facility's public

address system that guests must return to their rooms and stay there. Proper authorities, including the Stewards, have been notified and should arrive within a week.

Guests must remain in their quarters. Meals (and any desired deliverable services, such as massages) are will be brought to them by resort staff. The guests can call up entertainment (such as shows and games) on the consoles in their rooms. No one can leave the resort, as huge blast doors seal off the docking bays. These doors are controlled from the server room (area **B12**) and can't be physically forced opened without exerting a massive amount of effort that would draw plenty of attention.

Resort security disconnects the core computer servers from outside networks. As a result, no message or communication can be sent or received. In addition, security physically disconnects the servers housing proprietary Paradise Resorts data—guest lists, medical records, and so on—from the resort's network. Only general information, entertainment, and service operations remain accessible to guests and would-be hackers. This also removes any possibility of remotely disabling the docking bays' blast doors or Dr. Gragant's shadow signal.

When the initial announcement of the quarantine occurs, a few guests near the PCs—perhaps people they know—become rowdy. Security, already on edge, overreacts, drawing weapons and calling in a pair of security robots (see Creatures below). The PCs can attempt to defuse this situation. A PC who succeeds at a DC 22 Diplomacy or Intimidate check can convince the guests to cooperate. Alternatively, a PC who speaks with the security team and succeeds at a DC 25 Diplomacy check can convince them to go easy on the rowdy guests. If the PCs don't successfully intervene, security roughly escorts the rowdy guests to their quarters. No one is badly hurt in the process, though some harsh words are thrown about and one or two of the guests acquire some nasty bruises.

Any PCs who refuse to go to their quarters face the same security specialists and robots (see Creatures below). If the PCs resist and appear to be winning, more specialists show up to subdue them, including Kane Zaphol (see page 38 for stats, but exclude his eerie perception ability). Zaphol shows little mercy, and he is especially harsh to PCs he dislikes. Characters who must be subdued are locked in their rooms (Engineering DC 30 to bypass).

**Creatures:** A pair of New Elysium security specialists and a pair of patrol-class security robots attempt to enforce the quarantine, ushering guests to their quarters. They try to be polite, but are clearly on edge and all too ready to subdue anyone who refuses to budge.

### PATROL-CLASS SECURITY ROBOTS (2)    CR 4
**XP 1,200 each**
**HP** 52 each (*Starfinder Alien Archive* 94)

### NEW ELYSIUM SECURITY SPECIALISTS (2)    CR 5
**XP 1,600 each**
**HP** 70 each (see page 23)

**Story Award:** If the PCs help defuse the situation with unruly guests, award them 5,600 XP, as if they had defeated the security specialists and the security robots in combat.

## EVENT 10: MESSAGES AND VISIONS
On the morning of the twelfth day, Romi uses their personal comm to contact a PC they have bonded with or who was the most friendly. Romi asks if the PCs can send them a copy of the Keys to Elysium app. They mention that they and Indigo-13 were invited to the resort with the express purpose of acting as a "control group," not using the program to see if that affected their enjoyment of the facilities in any way. Romi says that with the quarantine, they are having some difficulty accessing

PATROL-CLASS
SECURITY ROBOT

certain entertainment in their room and that the app can no longer be downloaded from the server. A PC who succeeds at a DC 28 Sense Motive check can tell that Romi is lying. If pressed, Romi admits they want to look at the program's code, but refuse to say any more. If the PCs don't share the app with Romi, they are able to get it from another guest.

This interaction might prompt the PCs to examine the app closer themselves. See pages 10–11 for details on how they can analyze (and possibly remove) Keys to Elysium, but at this point, no staff respond when it is turned off or tampered with.

That night, Romi calls the PCs again. The PCs have an uneasy feeling of déjà vu as the android relates the following.

"Surely you've noticed the others acting strangely the past few days. Perhaps you have felt odd compulsions. If you haven't, you should take a look at this." The message cuts to a vidfeed showing the Painted Forest Playroom, where security specialists skirmish with guests, many of them with odd wounds, terrifying grins on their faces, and tears of blood streaming down their cheeks. Silent alarms flash in the background and text scrolls across the bottom of the feed that reads, 'Alert: unauthorized weapon discharge.' The message shows similar incidents occurring in the Hall of Splendors and Green Fields.

Romi returns. "There's some kind of... signal coming up from the abandoned mines beneath the resort, and it is disturbing people's minds. Indigo-13 and I are heading down there to investigate, but we need your help. If you avoid the main rooms, you probably won't run into any trouble. We've shut off the fan and opened the door. Please follow." The communication ends abruptly.

The PC who has the highest Wisdom score suddenly remembers all this occurring in a recent nightmare and feels a sense of impending doom; if this PC has any shadow corruption manifestations, she is more excited by this revelation than afraid. Until they find Romi, the PCs receive intermittent location information from the android's comm unit.

When the PCs leave their rooms to aid Romi, the corridor is dim and empty. Ask the last PC into the hall to attempt a Will saving throw. No matter the result, a flickering light attracts her attention in a direction opposite the one the PCs are headed. When she turns to look, she sees Teodhor just long enough to meet his unnerving gaze (see page 60). The lights then go out in that section of hallway. Teodhor flees into a side hall, using *shadow body* if he needs to. Try to play this off as another phantasm, as the PCs aren't destined to come face-to-face with the cantor just yet.

The PCs can use the spiral stairs or an elevator to reach the lower level. Remember that the stairs leading down to the facilities level are locked (Engineering DC 30 to bypass the lock). Any elevator the PCs use won't descend to the facilities level unless the PCs override the lockout with a successful DC 30 Computers or Engineering check. If the PCs exit an elevator, or even just pass one, they notice the light above another elevator blink, as if an elevator car were arriving at their floor. The doors open to reveal a dark and empty shaft.

If the PCs pass through the main floor of the resort, they can hear the sounds of combat—weapon discharge, screams, etc.—echoing from the various rooms and shops. If they seek out the source of these noises, the find only the remnants of various struggles—smears of blood, empty batteries, and the occasionally dead guest or resort staff.

As the PCs move through the hallways, Tok, who has been sneaking around taking footage of the quarantined resort, sees them and starts to trail them. Spotting him (or hearing a door open for him) requires a successful DC 26 Perception check. A PC who succeeds at this check spots only a small, dark form darting behind them to avoid notice, evocative of Teodhor; success by 5 or more is necessary to properly identify the ysoki. If he can keep out of sight, Tok shadows the PCs into the mines. If discovered, he begs the PCs to take him with them so he can record what happens. If Tok accompanies the PCs, he avoids danger and films the next encounters rather than fighting.

**Story Award:** For moving through the hallways of the resort and avoiding conflict, award the PCs 1,600 XP.

## EVENT 11: UNSEEN REVEALED (CR 8)

When the PCs arrive on New Elysium's lower level, they find it quiet and dimly lit. They continue to hear small arms fire and cries of pain echoing throughout the hallways. Romi and Indigo-13 left the northwestern door to the tech workshop (area **B11**) unlocked and the fans inside leading to the cooling tunnel deactivated.

**Creatures:** As the PCs enter the tech workshop, they find Rhissona Avran, fully under the sway of the shadow signal and partially transformed back into her reptoid form. She has three similarly corrupted guests with her, their casual vacation-wear stained with blood and oil and their skin marred with self-inflicted wounds. Read or paraphrase the following.

Rhissona Avran raises her gaze from a small, bloody orb in her palm. One of her eyes is a gory socket with optic fiber dangling from it, and the other is wide and glossy black. Her face seems to ripple between pale verthani skin and dark green scales. She cries out, "It's... it's on the inside! Is it... inside you? Can... can I see it? I must see it!"

She then attacks, ordering the corrupted guests to capture the PCs "for examination." The guests grab twisted pieces of furniture and sports equipment that function as makeshift clubs.

| CORRUPTED GUESTS (3) | CR 3 |
|---|---|

**XP 800 each**
NE Medium humanoid (human)
**Init** +6; **Perception** +8

**DEFENSE**        **HP** 48 each
**EAC** 14; **KAC** 16
**Fort** +7; **Ref** +5; **Will** +2
**Resistances** cold 5

**OFFENSE**
**Speed** 30 ft.
**Melee** club +11 (1d6+4 B)

**TACTICS**
**During Combat** The corrupted guests batter the PCs with their improvised weapons, hissing how "she will show us the way" and that the PCs "will soon know the truest pleasures." When a PC looks close to 0 Hit Points, the guests switch to dealing nonlethal damage (taking a –4 penalty to their attack rolls) to that PC.
**Morale** The corrupted guests fight to the death.

**STATISTICS**
**Str** +1; **Dex** +2; **Con** +4; **Int** +0; **Wis** +0; **Cha** +0
**Skills** Acrobatics +8, Athletics +8, Intimidate +13, Mysticism +8
**Languages** Common
**Other Abilities** shadow manifestations (coldblooded*)
**Gear** club
*See "Corrupted by Shadows" on page 40.

### RHISSONA AVRAN     CR 6
**XP 2,400**
Female reptoid master (*Alien Archive* 92)
**HP** 77

**TACTICS**
**During Combat** Rhissona uses her mental powers to attempt to subdue the PCs, lashing out with her claws if they get too close to her.
**Morale** Rhissona now takes pleasure from pain, so she fights until she is killed.

**STATISTICS**
**Other Abilities** shadow manifestations (pain refuge*)
*See "Corrupted by Shadows" on page 40.

**Development:** When Rhissona dies or is knocked unconscious, she reverts fully to her reptoid form. If the PCs interrogate her, it is clear that her mind is broken. She babbles incoherently about "the shadow of pain" that has fallen over the resort and of some unnamed "her" that is the center of the reptoid's fixations. If the PCs cast *speak with dead* on her corpse, her answers are a little more coherent, but all she knows is that something has corrupted

RHISSONA AVRAN

the minds of the resort's guests and staff. She truthfully notes that the current situation has nothing to do with the reptoids or their plans.

## THE MINES
When the PCs arrive at area **B14**, they find the northern blast door hanging open, leading to a dark tunnel that slopes sharply downward and splits off into several similar-looking passages. There is no light within the mines, and the air within is stale but breathable.

The PCs must continually ping Romi's comm unit in order to navigate the mines to find them and Indigo-13. When the PCs first enter the mines, and after every encounter below, each PC must attempt a skill check. The DC for this skill check is 26, and each PC can decide to use Computers (to track Romi's comm unit), Engineering (to assess the stability of the tunnels), Perception (to spot minor hazards), Physical Science (to note changes in the asteroid strata), or an appropriate Profession (such as archaeologist or miner), though at least one PC must attempt the Computers check each round. Each set of checks represents half an hour of moving through the tunnels, and the group succeeds if at least half of the PCs succeed at their checks. However, each failure adds 10 minutes to the total time, representing the group having to backtrack, move cautiously for a time, or help a comrade out of a minor danger. If the party fails (by more than half of the PCs failing their checks), it is at a disadvantage going into the next encounter, as noted in each encounter's description.

Tok continues to tag along with the PCs if they let him, and he tails them stealthily if they don't. The cantor Teodhor also follows the PCs into the mine. If the PCs close the blast door behind them, they might hear it open again a few moments later at your discretion.

## D. SHADOW CHRYSALIS (CR 10)
A pair of mature tenebrous worms lives in the tunnels, keeping close to a cocoon that is about to hatch. The cocoon is attached to a pillar in the western portion of a large, open chamber, and exudes supernatural darkness (see page 59). If PCs are successful at navigating the mine, they come from the east or southeast, spot the unusual gloom ahead, and can approach cautiously. Otherwise, they

SIGNAL OF SCREAMS

CAMPAIGN OUTLINE

THE DIASPORA STRAIN

PART 1: TWILIGHT IN ELYSIUM

PART 2: WAKING NIGHTMARES

PART 3: PARTING THE GLOOM

CORRUPTED BY SHADOWS

HORROR CAMPAIGNS

ALIEN ARCHIVES

CODEX OF WORLDS

blunder into the area from the west, possibly blind to the fact that the tenebrous worms are slithering in from the east.

The map for this area is found on page 32.

**Creatures:** If Tok is tailing the PCs, one of the tenebrous worms slays him in the darkness. A blood-curdling scream interrupts the PCs' examination of the cocoon, while the other worm enters the chamber from the north. The first worm joins the fight 1d4 rounds later. Otherwise, both worms arrive simultaneously from opposite ends of the cavern. During the first round of combat, one worm bites Tok (if he accompanies the PCs), killing him, and the creature's acid dissolves his body into wisps of shadowy smoke in a matter of moments.

After 1d6 rounds of combat or if any damage is done to the cocoon, a fully formed gloomwing emerges and immediately attacks the PCs.

## GLOOMWING · CR 4

**XP 1,200**
**HP** 50 (see page 56)

### TACTICS

**During Combat** The gloomwing is disoriented from its emergence and attacks PCs within reach randomly.

**Morale** If reduced to fewer than 15 Hit Points, the gloomwing tries to flee.

## TENEBROUS WORMS (2) · CR 8

**XP 4,800 each**
**HP** 125 each (see page 59)

### TACTICS

**During Combat** The tenebrous worms aren't clever enough to work in tandem and end up attacking different PCs.

**Morale** The hungry worms fight to the death.

**Treasure:** The PCs can search Tok's body to find an enhanced camera scanner with a fitting that allows it to be worn on the head, along with a shotgun microphone (*Armory* 107), a datapad that functions as a tier 2 computer (with the miniaturization [light bulk], hardened, and self-charging upgrades, worth 500 credits), a static arc pistol, a flashlight, a laser microphone, a credstick with 2,000 credits on it (for bribes), and three batteries (20 charges each). If Tok was killed in the tunnels, the PCs can find his corpse with a successful DC 20 Perception check. The PCs can also harvest the gloomwing's chitin if they wish (see page 56).

## E. MINING MACHINE (CR 9)

A deactivated mining robot rests at an intersection of tunnels. The cantor Teodhor reached this area before the PCs and rigged the light panels and robot here to activate as soon as any other creature entered the chamber. If the PCs succeed at navigating the mine, they come from the south and spot the light panels before anything happens, granting them a +2 circumstance bonus on the Reflex saving throw to avoid becoming blinded (see Hazard below). Otherwise, the group comes in from one of the northern tunnels with no chance to prepare.

The map for this area appears on page 32.

**Hazard:** A click and a sudden hum precede the pair of light panels briefly flaring to life and then blowing out. The burst of light affects everyone in the room other than the robot, whose sensors were not yet active. Each creature must succeed at a DC 16 Reflex saving throw or be blinded for 1 round and dazzled for 1d3 rounds after that.

**Creatures:** The mining robot lurches forward to destroy the PCs. Thanks to Teodhor's meddling, it believes them to be unusual formations of rock.

| MINING ROBOT | CR 9 |
|---|---|

**XP 6,400**
**HP** 145 (see page 58)

**TACTICS**
**During Combat** The mining robot attacks the nearest creature.
**Morale** The mining robot fights until it is destroyed or it can't see any other creature.

**Treasure:** The robot's integrated weapons are extremely valuable, and both can be removed with a successful DC 27 Engineering check.

## FINAL CALL

While the PCs move between the previous encounter and this one, Romi calls them again.

"I am sorry. So sorry. We… we ran across some unusual life-forms. Oozes. Highly aggressive. Indigo-13 is dead. I am trapped. I… I do not believe I will be alive when you arrive. Please, for my Indi, stop whatever is happening here. You must go deeper! Please." A weapon discharge punctuates the end of the communication.

## F. DWARVEN BARRACKS (CR 9)

If the PCs succeed at their checks to navigate the mines, they spot the dim lights of the barracks as they approach from the northern tunnels. They discover the tar-like remains of two void oozes, which can be identified with a successful DC 30 Life Science check. A PC who fails this check by 5 or fewer recognizes the goo as the remnant of an ooze, but not the specific type. The northern wall of this structure, which is built into the rock, has a set of automatic doors that still function and broad windows that look into the barracks' main lounge, which is dimly lit due to the void ooze's aura. A PC can

spot a void ooze by succeeding at a Perception check opposed by the ooze's Stealth check.

If more than half the PCs fail their checks to navigate the mines, they come in from the southwest, and when they turn the corner nearest the structure, they trigger the automatic doors there, alerting the creatures within.

This structure is a sturdy barracks constructed by Ulrikka Clanholdings for miners here. A PC examining the area and succeeding at a DC 20 Engineering check can tell the structure has remained here, mostly neglected, for decades. The outer doors can be locked from the inside, making this a safe place to rest. If the PCs do so, Teodhor attempts to use his *nightmare* spell-like ability on one unlucky PC.

The map for this area appears on page 32.

**Creatures:** One void ooze rests in the main lounge amid fine black ash and Indigo-13's belongings (see Treasure below). When a fight begins, another ooze slithers out from the bunks to the east, where Romi perished.

| VOID OOZES (2) | CR 7 |
|---|---|

**XP 3,200 each**
**HP** 105 each (see page 61)

**Development:** When the oozes die, the light level returns to normal thanks to the two beacons Romi and Indigo-13 brought down into the mines. Romi, obviously dead from a self-inflicted head wound, can be found in one of the eastern bunkrooms. Indigo-13's body was turned to fine ash by the void oozes within the main lounge. Among Romi's equipment (see Treasure below) is their comm unit, which appears to be locked onto a strange signal emanating from deeper within the mines. Following this signal requires the same checks as following Romi (see page 29).

**Treasure:** Searching the various rooms of the barracks uncovers a self-heating pot (*Armory* 131) and a mk 3 culinary synthesizer (*Armory* 129), both of dwarven make. A cabinet holds a nearly empty bin containing 300 UPBs and a handwritten note in Dwarven that provides three synthesizer recipes—dwarven stout, dwarven whiskey, and spiced dwarven sausage. Indigo-13's gear includes a d-suit II, a tactical seeker rifle, an advanced semi-auto pistol, 40 longarm rounds, and 20 small arm rounds. Romi's gear includes a silver AbadarCorp travel suit, a thunderstrike sonic pistol, a battery, and their customized comm unit, a tier 3 computer (with the hardened, miniaturized [negligible bulk], range III, and self-charging upgrades, and a built-in motion detector). Romi wiped all personal data from the computer besides the background image, a recent picture of a smiling Indigo-13 and Romi.

ROMI

SIGNAL OF SCREAMS

CAMPAIGN OUTLINE

THE DIASPORA STRAIN

PART 1: TWILIGHT IN ELYSIUM

PART 2: WAKING NIGHTMARES

PART 3: PARTING THE GLOOM

CORRUPTED BY SHADOWS

HORROR CAMPAIGNS

ALIEN ARCHIVES

CODEX OF WORLDS

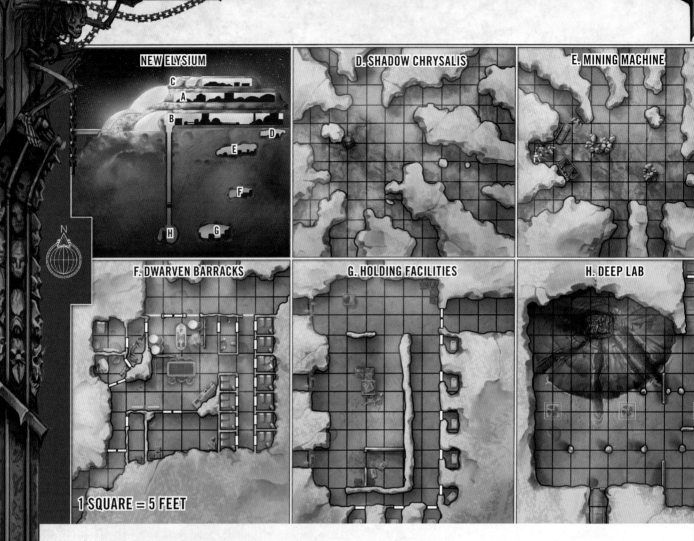

**NEW ELYSIUM**

C
A
B
D
E
F
H    G

N

**D. SHADOW CHRYSALIS**

**E. MINING MACHINE**

**F. DWARVEN BARRACKS**

**G. HOLDING FACILITIES**

**H. DEEP LAB**

1 SQUARE = 5 FEET

## G. HOLDING FACILITIES (CR 8)

As the PCs continue deeper into the mines, they find a facility intended for the storage of mining equipment that Dr. Gragant modified to hold her unwilling test subjects, turning it into a kind of prison. A trio of large airlock doors, now completely sealed with stone, are found along the western wall.

A map of this area is found above.

**Trap:** If the PCs succeeded at navigating the mine, they hear whispering as they enter. A character trained in Mysticism can attempt a DC 32 Mysticism check to sense the thinning between the Material Plane and the Shadow Plane here, granting that PC a +2 circumstance bonus to Mysticism checks to deal damage to the "trap" here. A PC who succeeds at the Perception check to notice the trap sees the outlines of fleeting apparitions and can warn others of the danger. If the PCs failed to navigate the mines, they will likely be caught by surprise when the apparitions manifest a few moments after the PCs enter the room.

In either case, the trap activates with the shrieks of several dying humanoids. These apparitions fill the area like a cloying fog, making the entire area difficult terrain and providing concealment for creatures more than 10 feet away from each other. The doors to the room seal shut and lock

(Computers DC 27 to bypass the locks or Engineering DC 27 to disable the lock). Then, apparitions of humanoids appear and grab at the PCs, clawing their flesh. These apparitions function as a mass of undead creatures. They have an EAC of 19, a KAC of 23, 120 Hit Points, and saving throw bonuses of +8. They have normal undead immunities, can be harmed by positive energy, and take half damage from nonmagical, non-area attacks. The apparitions are tied to this room, so they can't leave.

## TORTURED APPARITIONS                    CR 8
**XP 4,800**

**Type** magical; **Perception** DC 32; **Disable** Mysticism
DC 27 (a creature that succeeds at this check
calms the psychic feedback, dealing 30 damage to
the apparitions)

**Trigger** location (1-round onset); **Init** +14; **Duration** 1 minute;
**Reset** 24 hours

**Initial Effect** apparitions of tortured humanoids (shaken for
1d6 rounds); Will DC 18 negates; **Secondary Effect** fog
of ghosts (4d12 negative energy); Fortitude DC 18 half
(a creature that fails this saving throw by 5 or more is
also staggered for 1 round); multiple targets (all targets
in room)

**Treasure:** The area holds old containers, debris, and a few humanoid bones in the side chambers—the remains of a lashunta technician. On the skeleton, the PCs find a corona laser pistol with three batteries, *aura goggles* (*Alien Archive* 25), and an advanced medkit that contains three doses of sprayflesh and three *mk 2 serums of healing*.

## H. DEEP LAB (CR 9)

The remains of Dr. Gragant's lab are just a few hundred feet from the holding facilities, deep in the asteroid. As the PCs approach the area, the temperature drops to severe cold (*Core Rulebook* 400) and supernatural shadow prevents any source of nonmagical light from raising the light level above dim. Magical light raises the level of light normally. The PCs enter this area from the south and see a steel bulkhead in the rock. A burned-out control panel in the bulkhead is adjacent to an open doorway, misshapen as if something pulled the door from its frame and into the dark room beyond. When the PCs step into the ruined lab, read or paraphrase the following.

---

This room is a zone of devastation. White polycarbon plating has been twisted from the stone walls underneath, metal support pillars are buckled, and other structural elements are bent completely out of shape.

Everything bends toward a point in the far end of the room. There, amid a blackened, spherical hollow, is an enormous pile of crushed and warped structural material, furniture, machinery, and a security door alongside blackened humanoid bones. Several skulls of various species stare outward, their mouths open as if silently screaming. Frost covers this pile and the concavity around it. Debris made of crumbled material is thick around the heap.

Atop the pile, perhaps five feet from the ceiling and clutched in an upraised skeletal hand, is a tiny device like a personal comm unit with a single blinking light.

---

Another warped, open doorway leads north to a short hallway that ends in an unlocked elevator. Its doors power on and open automatically when approached, though the light inside is dim and flickering. The control panel inside has only two buttons: up and down. Pressing the down button does nothing, but pressing the up button takes the PCs to area **B15** of New Elysium.

As the PCs examine this area, whispering comes from all around, similar to that of the trap in area **G**. However, these murmurs address the PCs by name, requesting that they "join us in shadow," succumb to "delicious corruption," or serve as "new test subjects." Other voices speak of "witnessing the suffering" of the PCs or note that some of the characters are "quivering with anticipation." A PC who succeeds at a DC 26 Mysticism check can sense

that the Shadow Plane is very close here, focused on the grisly pile.

The map for this area appears on page 32.

**Creature:** The cantor Teodhor hides behind the pile of wreckage. If the PCs failed to navigate the mines to this area, he receives a +5 circumstance bonus to his Stealth checks to remain unseen. As the PCs approach the pile, he surreptitiously casts *paranoia* on one PC and then ducks back into hiding. He continues to use this ploy until confronted or he runs out of daily uses of that spell. He then attacks.

TORTURED APPARITION

## TEODHOR                                                        CR 9

**XP 6,400**

Male cantor (see page 60)

**HP** 120

### TACTICS

**During Combat** After exposing the PCs to his unnerving
gaze, Teodhor uses his waking nightmare ability. He
then fights with his claws, intermittently casting *lesser
confusion* or *paranoia*. Teodhor mocks the PCs and revels
in the pain they inflict upon him, giggling like a child.
When reduced to 60 or fewer Hit Points, he says that his
"dark lady's experiment here is already a success."

**Morale** Teodhor fights until the PCs reduce him to 30 Hit
Points or fewer. He then attempts to flee back into the
mines, casting *shadow body* if he can. Uninterested
in being killed, he harasses the PCs no further in
this adventure.

**Development:** Though Romi's comm unit points to
the device atop the 10-foot-tall pile as the source of the
shadow signal affecting New Elysium, that device actually
only masks the true source. A PC who examines the object
can determine this with a successful DC 22 Computers or
Engineering check. The Diminutive object can be destroyed
(AC 14, hardness 10, HP 10), but shutting it off requires no
check. When the PCs shut down the device, Romi's comm
unit beeps frantically for a few seconds as it recalibrates
before showing that the true broadcast emanates from far
above, somewhere within the resort.

## PART 3:
## PARTING THE GLOOM

While the PCs explored the mines, the fully corrupted
Buzzblades took over the resort's server room, guided by
whispers from Dr. Gragant. They have effectively killed Filip
Kallsner in the process, and now the frazzled Dr. Lominn is in
charge of the resort. She is at her wit's end and is holed up in
the staff lounge, evaluating her options.

The long elevator ride up from the mines to the resort is
eerily quiet. When they return to New Elysium's lower floor,
the PCs no longer hear the sounds of battle or the screams
of guests. The elevator opens onto a long and brightly lit
hallway that stands out from the rest of New Elysium by
its complete lack of decoration or other finishing touches.
The door at the northern end of the corridor is locked with
a physical lock (DC 33 Engineering to open) and leads to the
staff lounge (area **B9**).

## EVENT 12: MURDER IN THE LOUNGE (CR 9)

When the PCs open up the door and enter the staff lounge,
read or paraphrase the following.

The furniture of the staff lounge has been rearranged
haphazardly about the room to provide makeshift cover
against anything that might enter through the northern
door. Dr. Lominn and two security guards crouch behind
these barriers, startling when they hear a sound.

"Oh! It's you!" Dr. Lominn says, standing up with obvious
relief. "What are you doing? How did you get in there?"
Despite still being crisply dressed, she looks unwell. Her face
is pale and drawn with dark circles under her eyes, like she
hasn't slept in days. The guards look equally harried.

Suddenly, the lights flicker off. When they return a
moment later, the Buzzblade Zidhil stands behind Dr. Lominn,
his blade completely piercing her chest. Kofehsu, all four of
his arms outstretched, occupies the northern doorway.

"Come children, accept her embrace," the kasatha says, as
the two guards' eyes turn completely black.

The map for this area can be found on page 16.

**Creatures:** Kofehsu, Zidhil, and the two security specialists,
all fully corrupted by the shadow signal, attack the PCs.

## NEW ELYSIUM SECURITY SPECIALISTS (2)          CR 5

**XP 1,600 each**

**HP** 70 each (see page 23)

### TACTICS

**During Combat** The security specialists move to the other
sides of the barricades to gain cover.

**Morale** These specialists fight until they receive the sweet
release of death.

## KOFEHSU                                                      CR 5

**XP 1,600**

Male kasatha technomancer

LN Medium humanoid (kasatha)

**Init** +3; **Senses** darkvision 60 ft., low-light vision;
  Perception +11

### DEFENSE                                                      HP 60

**EAC** 16; **KAC** 17

**Fort** +4; **Ref** +4; **Will** +8

**Weaknesses** light blindness

### OFFENSE

**Speed** 30 ft.

**Technomancer Spells Known** (CL 5th; melee +10)
  2nd (3/day)—*daze monster* (DC 17), *invisibility*
  1st (6/day)—*grease* (DC 16), *jolting surge*, *magic missile*
  0 (at will)—*psychokinetic hand*, *token spell*

### TACTICS

**During Combat** Kofehsu casts *magic missile* a few times
  before moving into melee to cast *jolting surge*.

**Morale** Kofehsu fights to the death.

### STATISTICS

**Str** +2; **Dex** +3; **Con** +0; **Int** +5; **Wis** +0; **Cha** +0

**Skills** Acrobatics +16, Athletics +16, Computers +16,
  Culture +11, Mysticism +11

**Languages** Common, Kasatha

**Other Abilities** desert stride, four-armed, magic hacks (debug spell [1 die], harmful spells [+2 damage]), shadow manifestations (eerie perception*), spell cache (datapad)

**Gear** d-suit I, datapad

*See "Corrupted by Shadows" on page 40.

---

| ZIDHIL QUORIN | CR 5 |
|---|---|

**XP 1,600**

Male human soldier

LE Medium humanoid (human)

**Init** +7; **Perception** +11

**DEFENSE**            **HP** 70

**EAC** 17; **KAC** 19

**Fort** +7; **Ref** +5; **Will** +6; −2 vs. mind-affecting effects that aren't illusions or fear effects

**OFFENSE**

**Speed** 40 ft.

**Melee** *merciful yellow star flare axe* +14 (1d8+12 E & F; critical burn 1d8)

**Offensive Abilities** charge attack, fighting styles (blitz)

**TACTICS**

**During Combat** Zidhil charges the nearest PC, but he doesn't activate the *merciful* fusion on his weapon. He strikes at his chosen foe until that person has fallen.

**Morale** Zidhil fights to the death.

**STATISTICS**

**Str** +5; **Dex** +3; **Con** +2; **Int** +0; **Wis** +0; **Cha** +1

**Skills** Acrobatics +11, Athletics +16, Bluff +11, Intimidate +13

**Feats** Improved Combat Maneuver (bull rush, trip)

**Languages** Common

**Other Abilities** shadow manifestations (frightful*)

**Gear** d-suit I, *merciful yellow star flare axe*AR with 1 battery (20 charges)

*See "Corrupted by Shadows" on page 40.

**Treasure:** In addition to their foes' gear, the PCs can retrieve Dr. Lominn's personal datapad (a tier 3 computer with the hardened, miniaturized [light bulk], and self-charging upgrades, worth 4,500 credits). It is biometrically locked (see Development below).

**Development:** A PC must succeed at a DC 36 Computers check to bypass the biometric locks of Dr. Lominn's datapad. Taking her hand and placing it on the sensor grants a +5 circumstance bonus to this check. The PCs have three attempts at this check before the datapad locks out further attempts for 1 hour.

The datapad holds Dr. Lominn's everyday administrative records, along with her documentation of the progression of the "illness" within New Elysium. She notes that many guests and staff members, including Filip Kallsner, have experienced hallucinations (with some clear references to Teodhor), paranoia, and psychosomatic distress. The most recent entries note that all these symptoms have grown much worse: that guests are

fighting each other and security personnel, the Buzzblades have taken over the server room, and Filip disappeared into the air ducts. The datapad also has a map of the resort's facilities section and can serve as a key to access the server, although it can't do so remotely. Further, it contains access to the medical facilities' discretionary fund of 4,000 credits, which can be transferred from the datapad to a credstick or another account.

## FACILITIES EXPLORATION

Romi's comm unit can trace the true source of the shadow signal to the server room, right around the corner from the staff lounge. The corridor between the two areas is a gory scene of slain security specialists who faced off against the Buzzblades and lost. The PCs need not go there directly and can explore the resort's lower level as much as they like.

# EVENT 13: BUZZBLADES BRAWL (CR 10)

The door to the server room is now unlocked.

---

Cool air blows through this dimly lit room. Banks of computer nodes behind rounded transparent doors occupy most of the chamber. Several lights in the eastern part of the room flicker on, revealing an alcove that contains Filip hanging limply from several sets of chains. He is shirtless and patches of skin have been expertly and bloodlessly peeled from his body.

---

Illumination from the racks of servers provides dim light. A PC who succeeds at a DC 25 Medicine check or DC 30 Perception check can see from afar that Filip is still breathing, albeit shallowly.

**Creatures:** Now fully corrupted, Beryldor, Lomer, Virlae, and Yazeloya hide here behind the servers. They wait for a few rounds or until the PCs get closer to Filip, whichever comes first. Yazeloya emerges from behind a node near Filip, dragging her chain behind her. "There's nothing here for you," she says. "Nothing but pain." The Buzzblades then attack.

During the fight, Filip stirs. At first, his eyes widen and he screams. Then, focused on the distance, he comments on the battle, speaking of some unknown female patron. For instance, if Yazeloya scores a critical hit, Filip says, "She is pleased. Oh, truly, you are her instrument." Once per round, whenever he does this, it inspires one Buzzblade, allowing that NPC to ignore one of the following conditions for 1 round: confused, fascinated, fatigued, shaken, sickened, or staggered.

The PCs can try to free Filip while the battle rages, but it is difficult. Not only does Yazeloya try to stop anyone from approaching him, but releasing him from the chains that restrain one of his limbs requires a full action and a successful DC 21 Strength check. This must be done four times to completely free him, whereupon he slumps to the ground and continues to inspire the Buzzblades. Any attempt to deal damage to the chains damages Filip instead. However, he reacts to this pain as if it were pleasure. He (and the chains) have an AC of 5 and 25 Hit Points. If he is killed, see Development on page 37.

SIGNAL OF SCREAMS

CAMPAIGN OUTLINE

THE DIASPORA STRAIN

PART 1: TWILIGHT IN ELYSIUM

PART 2: WAKING NIGHTMARES

PART 3: PARTING THE GLOOM

CORRUPTED BY SHADOWS

HORROR CAMPAIGNS

ALIEN ARCHIVES

CODEX OF WORLDS

## LOMER                                          CR 5

**XP 1,600**

**HP** 70 (see page 24)

### STATISTICS

**Other Abilities** shadow manifestations (shadow cloak*)

*See "Corrupted by Shadows" on page 40.

## VIRLAE NILUFEH                                 CR 5

**XP 1,600**

**HP** 70 (see page 24)

### STATISTICS

**Other Abilities** shadow manifestations (shadow cloak*)

* See "Corrupted by Shadows" on page 40.

## BERYLDOR RENDRUMM                              CR 5

**XP 1,600**

Male dwarf soldier

LE Medium humanoid (dwarf)

BERYLDOR RENDRUMM

**Init** +3; **Senses** darkvision 60 ft.; **Perception** +11

### DEFENSE                                       HP 70

**EAC** 17; **KAC** 19

**Fort** +7; **Ref** +5; **Will** +6; −2 vs. mind-affecting effects that aren't illusions or fear effects, +2 vs. poison, spells, and spell-like abilities

**Defensive Abilities** guard's protection, slow but steady

### OFFENSE

**Speed** 30 ft.

**Melee** *merciful tactical swoop hammer* +14 (1d10+12 B; critical knockdown)

**Offensive Abilities** fighting styles (guard), traditional enemies

### TACTICS

**During Combat** Beryldor remains close to Yazeloya, using his reaction to soak up damage dealt to her. He doesn't activate his *merciful* fusion.

**Morale** Beryldor fights to the death.

### STATISTICS

**Str** +5; **Dex** +3; **Con** +2; **Int** +0; **Wis** +0; **Cha** +1

**Skills** Acrobatics +11, Athletics +16, Bluff +11, Intimidate +13

**Feats** Improved Combat Maneuver (bull rush)

**Languages** Common

**Other Abilities** armor training, shadow manifestations (frightful*)

**Gear** d-suit I, *merciful tactical swoop hammer*

*See "Corrupted by Shadows" on page 40.

## YAZELOYA GOLKAMI                               CR 8

**XP 4,800**

Female vesk soldier

LE Medium humanoid (vesk)

**Init** +8; **Senses** low-light vision; **Perception** +16

### DEFENSE                                      HP 125

**EAC** 21; **KAC** 23

**Fort** +10; **Ref** +8; **Will** +9; +2 vs. fear

### OFFENSE

**Speed** 40 ft.

**Melee** acolyte shadow chains +19 (3d4+17 C; critical bind) or unarmed strike +19 (1d3+21 B)

**Offensive Abilities** charge attack, fighting styles (blitz), gear boosts (flash freeze)

### TACTICS

**During Combat** Yazeloya attempts to intimidate PCs using her frightful manifestation and charges demoralized foes.

**Morale** The valiant brutaris champion fights to the death.

### STATISTICS

**Str** +6; **Dex** +4; **Con** +2; **Int** +0; **Wis** +0; **Cha** +2

**Skills** Athletics +21, Intimidate +16

**Feats** Close Combat[PW]

**Languages** Common, Vesk

**Other Abilities** shadow manifestations (frightful*)

**Gear** advanced lashunta tempweave (*haste circuit*), acolyte shadow chains[AR]

* See "Corrupted by Shadows" on page 40.

**Development:** When Filip dies or the battle ends in the PCs' favor, read or paraphrase the following.

---

"Oh, I see you, dark lady," says Filip, bloody tears rolling down his cheeks in something akin to ecstasy. "Your embrace awaits." His eyes close, and he gasps. His bones crack, breaking like twigs as his body folds in on itself. He disappears into a whispering mote of shadow that vanishes with a sigh.

---

This disappearance takes but a few seconds. The temperature of the alcove is reduced to extreme cold for the next minute. With no further interference, the PCs can shut down the resort's servers and stop the shadow signal.

## EVENT 14: SHUTTING DOWN THE SERVERS (CR 7)

New Elysium's servers function as a tier 5 computer with numerous modules that control the resort's facilities. Without Dr. Lominn's datapad, gaining basic access to the servers requires a successful DC 33 Computers check.

Basic access allows the PCs to view only the resort's schematics and basic personnel information, as well as a note that the resort is currently under quarantine with lockdown protocols in place that seal off the docking bays. In addition, the PCs can see that the servers are connected to three data modules: financial, security, and an unnamed module (which contains information about Dr. Gragant's shadow signal). Gaining access to the first two data modules requires a successful DC 33 Computers check, but using Lominn's datapad grants a +4 circumstance bonus to the check to access the security data module. The unnamed module is behind a firewall and requires a successful DC 35 Computers check to access.

The financial data module has a lockout countermeasure that blocks access for 4 hours after three failed access attempts. The security data module has an alarm that goes off after a single failed attempt to access it, but no one is around to answer it. The information within each data module is listed below.

**Trap:** The unnamed module is protected by a trap that triggers after one failed attempt to access it. Those affected by the countermeasure's curse experience one phantasm each day until the curse is removed. The saving throw DC for these phantasms is 17, and they grant no XP.

| HACKER'S SHADOW CURSE | CR 7 |
|---|---|

**XP 3,200**

**Type** hybrid; **Perception** DC 30; **Disable** Computers DC 25 (rewrite virus code) or Mysticism DC 25 (dispel curse)
**Trigger** touch; **Reset** 1 minute
**Effect** curse (target experiences up to one phantasm per day; this is a curse effect); Will DC 17 negates; multiple targets (all creatures within server room)

**Financial Module:** This module contains fiscal records for the resort going back 7 years, from the planning stages of

the resort until now. Among other mundane topics, such as gambling ledgers, these records reveal contracts Paradise Resorts signed allowing Eclipse Innovations to automate this facility 4 years ago. A hacker with access to Dr. Lominn's datapad can convince the system to transfer her latest pay and bonus (2,500 credits) to an outside account with a successful DC 25 Computers check.

**Security Module:** Gaining access to the security data module allows characters to observe the security feeds, which show several gruesome scenes across the resort, along with people fighting or doing other terrible, irrational things. External cameras show the docking bays are clear of danger and that the PCs' ship (or a vessel they can commandeer) is ready to depart. More importantly, the security module allows the PCs to deactivate the quarantine lockdown on the docking bays. Doing so opens the blast doors that lead there.

**Shadow Module:** The unnamed module controls the shadow signal that permeates New Elysium. Gaining access to it allows the PCs to finally shut it down. In addition, the module contains many notes that refer to the resort and the Keys to Elysium app as a "test project," with references to a larger project called the "Penumbra Protocol" in development on Verces in the city of Cuvacara. It identifies Kaeon Rhyse as the Eclipse Innovations executive in charge of this project, and mentions a mysterious other person or entity providing "necessary backing and encouragement." At this point, the PCs can research Eclipse Innovations further if they haven't already (see page 11).

**Story Award:** The PCs gain 1,600 XP for ending the quarantine lockdown and 1,600 XP more for learning about the shadow signal and shutting it down.

## EVENT 15: FINAL CHASE (CR 9)

At this point, the PCs will probably want to escape from New Elysium. They face no further opposition as they pass through the staff area, but at some point as they move through the resort's main floor (but before they reach Green Fields), they are accosted by a corrupted Kane Zaphol.

---

"If it isn't the troublemakers!" says Kane Zaphol, lurching forward. Symmetrical, bloody gashes line his cheeks and forehead. His eyes are glossy black and surrounded with gray veins. His armor is damaged and dotted with gore. He makes a sweeping motion with both hands, one of which holds a grenade. "Where do you think you're going?"

---

Wherever this encounter takes place, the lights begin to flicker, providing only dim light.

**Creatures:** A moment later, Kane hurls his grenade at the PCs with a scream and activates two nearby security robots.

As the fight proceeds, the noise attracts several corrupted guests. Every round after the first, these unfortunates arrive in howling groups of 1d3–1 (minimum 0) from all directions. Only four should be present at any one time, and they randomly attack the nearest targets.

SIGNAL OF SCREAMS

CAMPAIGN OUTLINE

THE DIASPORA STRAIN

PART 1: TWILIGHT IN ELYSIUM

PART 2: WAKING NIGHTMARES

PART 3: PARTING THE GLOOM

CORRUPTED BY SHADOWS

HORROR CAMPAIGNS

ALIEN ARCHIVES

CODEX OF WORLDS

Put pressure on the PCs to retreat, and don't block all the exits. If they refuse to escape, do your best to make it clear they're slowly being overwhelmed. When they do run, Kane Zaphol (if he is still alive) and a trio of corrupted guests chase them. Any surviving security bots remain behind, trying to subdue other guests. Each round as they flee, 1d4–2 (minimum 0) more corrupted guests join the chase toward Green Fields and the nearby docks.

## CORRUPTED GUESTS             CR 3
**XP 800 each**
**HP** 48 each (see page 28)

## PATROL-CLASS SECURITY ROBOTS (2)    CR 4
**XP 1,200 each**
**HP** 52 each (*Alien Archive* 94)

## KANE ZAPHOL             CR 6
**XP 2,400**
Male human soldier
LE Medium humanoid (human)
**Init** +5; **Senses** darkvision 60 ft., low-light vision; **Perception** +13

### DEFENSE           HP 90
**EAC** 18; **KAC** 21
**Fort** +8; **Ref** +6; **Will** +7

### OFFENSE
**Speed** 30 ft., fly 30 ft. (jetpack, average)
**Melee** aurora shock pad +14 (2d4+9 E; critical staggered [DC 16])
**Ranged** static arc rifle +16 (1d12+6 E; critical arc 1d6) or
flash grenade II +16 (explode [10 ft., blinded 1d4 rounds, DC 16])
**Offensive Abilities** fighting styles (hit-and-run), nimble fusillade, opening volley

### TACTICS
**During Combat** Kane attacks with abandon, focusing on any PC he has decided he dislikes due to earlier interactions.
**Morale** Kane sees this situation as kill or be killed.

### STATISTICS
**Str** +3; **Dex** +5; **Con** +2; **Int** +0; **Wis** +0; **Cha** +1
**Skills** Athletics +18, Diplomacy +13, Intimidate +13, Sense Motive +13
**Feats** Mobility
**Languages** Common, Vercite
**Other Abilities** shadow manifestations (eerie perception*)

KANE ZAPHOL

**Gear** estex suit III (aurora shock pad^AR with 1 battery [20 charges], jetpack), static arc rifle with 2 high-capacity batteries (40 charges each), flash grenade II, binders
*See "Corrupted by Shadows" on page 40.

**Story Award:** Grant the PCs 6,400 XP for this encounter, even if they flee from Kane and no matter how many corrupted guests they defeat.

## BLOOD FIELDS
As the PCs flee toward the docking bays while being chased by Kane and the corrupted guests, they pass by Green Fields. They can see that bodies litter the park, and the waterfall runs red with the blood of guests and staff. However, not all within Green Fields are dead.

Several more corrupted guests within Green Fields notice the PCs and come charging, screaming and howling. Simultaneously, Vorilynn, who has been hiding among the park's foliage, emerges. Already injured, dirty, and bleeding, she cries out in terror and also runs toward the PCs. A PC who succeeds at a DC 25 Sense Motive check realizes she is only afraid and probably uncorrupted. Otherwise, the PCs have only a split second to react before she is on them. If any PC attacks her and hits an AC of 17, the injury is fatal—Vorilynn looks shocked as she falls, and the PCs immediately comprehend she wasn't corrupted. Alternatively, an NPC, such as Kane Zaphol, mortally wounds Vorilynn with an attack before she can reach the group. Her dying act is to cast *fog cloud*, providing the PCs enough concealment to get to the docking bays.

## EVENT 16: DOGFIGHT (CR 8)
When the PCs reach the docking bays, they find their vessel ready and fully upgraded. If the PCs arrived at New Elysium on a Ringworks Sentinel instead, they find the tier 8 starship the players designed (see page 8). This starship's security is down and anyone can activate its computers. The previous owners became corrupted during their stay. The PCs might find a few personal effects of this previous crew, possibly recognizing them among the dead within the resort.

Either way, it takes a few minutes to warm up the engines. During that time, a few more guests and Kane Zaphol, if he has survived, rush into the docking bay.

SIGNAL OF
SCREAMS

CAMPAIGN
OUTLINE

THE DIASPORA
STRAIN

PART 1:
TWILIGHT IN
ELYSIUM

PART 2:
WAKING
NIGHTMARES

PART 3:
PARTING THE
GLOOM

CORRUPTED
BY
SHADOWS

HORROR
CAMPAIGNS

ALIEN
ARCHIVES

CODEX OF
WORLDS

They can enter the resort's boarding airlock, but they can't breach the ship. When the PCs pull away from the dock, these unfortunates are ejected from the resort into open space.

**Starship Combat:** As the PCs leave the asteroid, two of New Elysium's patrol vessels, the *Harp* and the *Lute*, linger nearby. A message from one of the vessels warns the PCs they are violating quarantine and orders them to return to the docking bay. Before the PCs can explain themselves, the other vessel fires a blast from its gravity gun at their ship, immediately followed by an unnerving cackle. It is clear that the shadow signal has corrupted even those outside of the resort.

The Sentinel crews act erratically, broadcasting messages that alternate between official-sounding orders to cease hostilities and barely comprehensible rants about the coming "queen of shadow." There is a 25% chance each round that each crew member does nothing.

The PCs need only escape the area. If they are ever more than 15 hexes from a Sentinel and the pilot does nothing that round, that Sentinel has abandoned the chase.

### HARP AND LUTE                                        TIER 5

Ringworks Sentinels (see inside front cover)
**HP** 65 each

**Story Award:** If the PCs defeat or outrun the Sentinels, award them 4,800 XP

## CONCLUDING
## THE ADVENTURE

Though the PCs are free of New Elysium, they aren't cured of any shadow corruption they might have contracted. This corruption stays dormant (unless the PCs have already given into it) and is incurable until the PCs slay Dr. Gragant at the end of the Signal of Screams Adventure Path. A PC who casts *detect affliction* and succeeds at a DC 25 Mysticism check can determine the nature of the corruption, but not how to remove it. Until then, the only lead they have to follow is the fact that Eclipse Innovations is involved and they could be attempting to repeat this process in Cuvacara on Verces. The planet is only 1d6 days away via Drift travel or 1d6+2 days away using standard thrusters.

A PC who succeeds at a DC 15 Culture check intuits that involving the authorities is likely to result in a slow response. If the PCs try to contact such persons anyway, such as the Stewards, they learn that news of New Elysium's quarantine never left the resort. While the contacted officials might believe what the PCs are saying, they require at least a few weeks to gather solid evidence.

The PCs are on their own.

# CORRUPTED BY SHADOWS

"Each of us contains seeds of darkness, waiting to take purchase in the soil of the psyche and be watered with the tears of pain. Even the saintliest priests and the most charitable philanthropists have hearts that harbor slivers of shadow, but they would never admit it to others or themselves. We are far more enlightened. We embrace these shadows, not because we are evil, but because we are alive. To deny an aspect of one's nature is to deny reality."

—Juliran Ashgate, priest of Zon-Kuthon

Corruption is an insidious affliction of the soul. A number of different corruptions exist, from the mind-rending horror of ghostly possession to the monstrous physical transformation of lycanthropy. However, all corruptions function in a similar way. When a character first contracts a corruption, it shows itself in minor symptoms—brief bouts of melancholy or a mild fixation on unusual stimuli or a particular environment. The corruption eats away at the victim's mind and spirit with the promise of dark gifts that come with frightful drawbacks. Fighting these temptations is draining on a victim, and some spend their entire lives on the verge of giving in. Others believe they can control their corruption, and allow the corruption to progress in order to gain the power it grants. Such beings eventually become completely defiled as corruption takes a permanent hold over them.

The following pages describe how corruption affects a Starfinder character, starting with general rules. Then shadow corruption, which is used in the Signal of Screams Adventure Path, is provided as a fleshed-out example. Finally, other possible corruptions are described.

## CONTRACTING CORRUPTION

A character can contract corruption in numerous ways, from an ancient curse to a technomagical virus. A corruption's origin is usually supernatural, and contracting one requires failing a saving throw against the corruption's cause. When corruption first takes hold, it begins at stage 1 and is dormant. A victim might not grasp the nature of the affliction for some time. During this period, dark urges or horrific nightmares might occur, but nothing more.

## CORRUPTION PROGRESS

When you're afflicted with a corruption, you must attempt a saving throw against the corruption's progress at the end of each day, before taking the normal 8 hours of uninterrupted rest to regain spent Resolve Points and daily abilities. If the corruption is mental, this is a Will save. A physical corruption requires a Fortitude save. The save DC is equal to 10 + half your level + the number of manifestations you have (see below). If you fail, you can instead spend a number of Resolve Points equal to 1 + the number of manifestations you have in order to succeed. If you can't or don't spend the required number of Resolve Points, your corruption progresses one stage. Every time the corruption progresses to an even-numbered stage, such as from stage 1 (dormant) to stage 2, you gain a manifestation.

## MANIFESTATIONS

Corruptions become evident through manifestations, which alter your mind and body in strange ways. A manifestation grants a power, known as a gift, but it also imposes a detriment, known as a stain. When you gain a manifestation, you choose which manifestation to receive, but some have prerequisites that must be met before they can be selected.

## MYSTERIOUS MANIFESTATIONS

To increase the mystery of how corruption functions, you (as GM) can control the selection of manifestations available to PCs. You might offer a choice of two or three manifestations to a player whose PC has failed a saving throw against a corruption, describing the gifts in tempting detail but only hinting at the stains. In addition, you can forgo the default rules and control the rate at which manifestations can be gained. You might decide that a PC can gain no more than one manifestation per level, for example, slowing the progress of corruption and the increase in power it offers.

**Saving Throws:** Unless stated otherwise, for gifts that require a saving throw, the DC is equal to 10 + half your level + your key ability score modifier.

**Refusing Gifts:** When you select a manifestation, you can refuse its gift and accept only the stain. If you do, you gain a +1 bonus to further saving throws against that corruption. This bonus stacks for each gift you refuse. You can change your mind and accept a gift at any time, however, losing the corresponding bonus to saving throws against your corruption and risking your soul.

**Alterations:** The number of manifestations you have affects your personality and appearance, as detailed in a given corruption. If you accept five gifts or have nine manifestations, you succumb to corruption and become an NPC under the GM's control. This change can also alter your other statistics, depending on the corruption.

**Multiple Corruptions:** In the rare case that you gain multiple corruptions, you must attempt separate saving throws against each, and gain manifestations from each corruption you fail the saving throw against, in order. You still succumb to corruption when you have five gifts or nine manifestations, however, regardless of the source. Therefore, having multiple corruptions only speeds your doom. When a specific corruption's feature is based on the number of manifestations you have, you count only the manifestations that arise from that specific corruption.

## REMOVING A CORRUPTION

Corruptions are hard to remove. Each requires a specific set of deeds or circumstances as detailed in the corruption's description. *Remove affliction* can suppress the gifts and stains of a target's corruptions for 10 minutes per caster level. In addition, one casting of *break enchantment* or *remove affliction* can remove one manifestation, but only if the victim meets the cure conditions of the corruption or hasn't accepted the gift associated with that manifestation. The DC for such spells is 15 + three times the number of manifestations the target has. Removing a manifestation in this way doesn't cure the corruption.

# SHADOW CORRUPTION

Those who spend extended time on the Shadow Plane, are repeatedly exposed to shadow magic, or fall under the sway of creatures such as velstracs, certain undead, or shadowy fey, risk contracting shadow corruption. Shadow corruption is an affliction with the following parameters.

## SHADOW CORRUPTION

**Type** mental corruption; **Save** Will DC = 10 + half the victim's level + the number of manifestations the victim has; on a failure, a victim can spend a number of Resolve Points equal to 1 + the number of manifestations the victim has to succeed instead

**Frequency** 1/day

**Cure** Destroy the creature, object, or effect that caused the corruption, or the victim can purify themselves by spending 1 month spreading joy, experiencing joy, and living in the light of a habitable world's sunlight. At the end of each month spent this way, the victim can refuse a previously accepted gift, allowing *break enchantment* or *remove affliction* to remove the related manifestation. Using a gift from any corruption while undergoing purification means the victim has to start that month over.

When the corruption first takes hold, it's dormant but gives you regular nightmares. In these dreams, you walk through familiar places, but many of the details are subtly wrong. You feel like you're being watched from the shadows, a belief that lingers for a few moments after you wake. These visions don't affect your health, but they make you irritable or jumpy for an hour or so after you awaken. After a few days, sudden flashes of bright light cause you to flinch, and you start to catch glimpses of movement in the shadows out of the corner of your eye.

## SHADOW PROGRESSION

When you gain your first manifestation, your nightmares grow vivid, showing you individuals who have the faces of your loved ones but are wrapped in chains and hanging from the ceiling or walls, writhing in what might be pleasure or pain. You still feel as if something watches you in these dreams. During your waking hours, you can sometimes hear the jingling of the nightmare chains, especially when alone with your thoughts or in times of great stress. Sources of joy start to lose their appeal—colors are muted, sounds are muffled, smells and tastes are bland or bitter, a touch that doesn't bring extreme sensation might go unnoticed.

When you gain your second and third manifestations, feelings of being disconnected from the world increase dramatically. If you accepted your gifts, you feel this detachment enlightens you, and upon accepting your third gift, if your alignment is good, it shifts to neutral. Accepting your corruption by using its gifts makes your nightmares seem more like peaceful dreams, and you might attempt to recreate these dreams in the real world. To feel anything, you turn to pain and other extreme experiences. Forays into self-harm might be easy to hide from others, but your need for more slowly increases.

Once you accept your fourth gift, your normal emotions are nearly dead. Your greatest pleasure comes from causing harm and being harmed. You believe the corruption is a personal improvement and try to explain its benefits to others. If you see someone who has shadow corruption, you sense the affliction even if it's dormant. You focus on encouraging such people to give in to the darkness.

If you accept a fifth gift, the corruption takes complete control of you, and you become evil if you're not already. You undergo extreme body modifications and augmentations that cause consistent if not constant pain. You might believe yourself to be a prophet of pain, and you share this pain with others, perhaps killing them in the process. Alternatively, you could disappear into the Shadow Plane, where those like you, who watched you from your nightmares, wait to embrace you as one of their own.

## SHADOW MANIFESTATIONS

Possible manifestations of shadow corruption follow.

### COLDBLOODED

The chill of the deep shadows has inured you to cold.

**Gift:** You gain cold resistance 5. If you have three or more manifestations, this resistance increases to 10.

**Stain:** Your appearance becomes disturbing. Reduce your Charisma score by 1.

### COLDBLOODED TOUCH

Your touch is infused with the life-sapping gloom of the Shadow Plane.

**Prerequisites:** Coldblooded, one other manifestation.

**Gift:** As a standard action, you can make a melee attack against EAC that deals 2d4 cold damage for each manifestation you have. If you deal damage with this manifestation, the target must succeed at a Will saving throw or become unable to benefit from morale bonuses for 1 minute. You can use this manifestation a number of times per day equal to the number of manifestations you have.

**Stain:** Your body withers. Reduce your Strength, Dexterity, and Constitution scores by 1 point each.

### DEADENED EMOTIONS

You are hollow inside.

**Gift:** You gain a +2 insight bonus to Bluff checks and saving throws against mind-affecting effects. If another creature attempts to read your mind (such as with *detect thoughts*) and you succeed at the saving throw, you can render that creature shaken for 1 round as a reaction. You can do the same to a creature that fails a Bluff, Diplomacy, or Intimidate check against you by directing your lifeless gaze at it. This is a mind-affecting fear effect. A creature affected by your deadened emotions becomes immune to it for 24 hours.

**Stain:** Reduce any morale bonus you receive by 1.

## EERIE PERCEPTION

Your eyes turn dull gray, milky white, or glossy black, and you become more accustomed to the dark.

**Gift:** You gain low-light vision and darkvision with a range of 60 feet. If you already have darkvision, its range increases by 30 feet instead. In addition, if you are aware of a creature's location and that creature is hidden only due to dim light, darkness, or invisibility, you are considered to be observing that creature until it moves out of line of sight or successfully hides from you again.

**Stain:** You gain light blindness: you're blinded for 1 round when first exposed to bright light, and you are dazzled for as long as you remain in an area of bright light.

## FRIGHTFUL

Fear is another tool in your arsenal, and you use it skillfully.

**Gift:** You find joy in scaring others, and have a knack for knowing how to do so. You gain a +2 enhancement bonus to Intimidate checks, and the save DCs of your fear effects increase by 2. You can use Intimidate skill demoralize others as a move action.

**Stain:** Your mind is so focused on spreading fear that you are susceptible to mental manipulation. You take a –2 penalty to saving throws against mind-affecting effects that aren't illusions or fear effects, and you lose any bonuses against or immunities to such effects. If you fail a saving throw against such an effect, it lasts 1d3 additional rounds.

## FRIGHTFUL CRUELTY

You have learned how to hurt those who are afraid.

**Prerequisites:** Frightful.

**Gift:** Once per round, if you damage a creature that is shaken, frightened, panicked, or cowering, you deal extra damage equal to half your level. If you damage multiple fearful creatures with one attack or effect, choose only one of them to take this bonus damage.

**Stain:** You are off your game in combat until you hurt or scare someone. Therefore, you take a –2 penalty to

attack rolls and can't gain morale bonuses on your attack rolls until you deal damage to a significant foe or render someone shaken, frightened, panicked, or cowering.

## INSUBSTANTIALITY

Your corporeal form can flicker into insubstantial shadow.

**Prerequisites:** Two other manifestations.

**Gift:** You have a 20% chance to treat a critical hit as a normal hit, allowing you to ignore the critical hit's extra damage and critical hit effect. If the attack affects incorporeal creatures normally, such as a weapon with the *ghost killer* fusion, you can't ignore it in this way.

**Stain:** If an ally targets you with a beneficial spell that has a range of touch, you have a 20% chance to gain no benefit from it. The spell is still cast and expended.

## PAIN REFUGE

The lines between pleasure and pain are blurred for you.

**Gift:** The first time you take Hit Point damage in a given combat, for 1 round you can roll attack rolls, saving throws, and skill checks twice and take the better result. You can do so again the first time you drop below half your Hit Points in a given combat. During this time, however, you can't benefit from morale bonuses.

**Stain:** Increase any damage you take by an amount equal to the number of manifestations you have, up to a maximum of double the original amount of damage.

## PAINFUL CLARITY

Pain clears your mind.

**Prerequisites:** Pain Refuge.

**Gift:** As a reaction when you fail a saving throw against a mind-affecting effect, you can use a weapon you're wielding to deal yourself 4 damage, subtracted directly from your Hit Points. If you do so, you can reroll the saving throw. This benefit has no effect if you reduce the damage you inflict on yourself by any amount.

**Stain:** You thrive on pain, and thus you always have a number of self-inflicted wounds. Reduce your maximum Hit Points by a number equal to half your level.

## SHADOW CLOAK

You easily blend in with shadows.

**Gift:** Provided you are in an area of dim light or darkness, you can use Stealth to hide even while being observed.

**Stain:** Your muscles weaken. When you attempt any Strength-based check, roll twice and take the worse result.

## SHADOW JAUNT

You can jump from shadow to shadow with little effort.

**Prerequisites:** One other manifestation.

**Gift:** As a full action, you can teleport, as if using a *dimension door* spell, from one area of dim light or darkness to another, transporting only yourself and objects you wear or carry. If you are overburdened, this teleportation fails. Further, you can teleport only up to 60 feet. Once you teleport, you can't do so again until you take a 10-minute rest during which you could regain Stamina Points. You can use this ability a number of times per day equal to the number of manifestations you have.

**Stain:** You are apathetic and difficult to stir into action. When you roll your initiative check, roll twice and take the worse result.

## UNNERVING GAZE

With a glance, you can fill your foes with regret for their wasted potential.

**Prerequisites:** Frightful, one other manifestation.

**Gift:** You gain a gaze attack that causes foes within 30 feet of you to become shaken for 1d3 rounds unless they succeed at a Will saving throw. As a swift action, you can suppress or reactivate this ability, which is a mind-affecting fear effect. A creature that succeeds at the saving throw is immune to your unnerving gaze for 24 hours.

**Stain:** You have an unsettling aura. When you attempt a Bluff or Diplomacy check, roll twice and take the worse result. It also takes you twice as long to use the gather information task of the Diplomacy skill.

## VELSTRAC DURABILITY

Infused with shadow, you take on a trait of the velstracs.

**Prerequisites:** Pain Refuge, Painful Clarity.

**Gift:** You gain an amount of damage reduction equal to twice the number of manifestations you have. Good-aligned weapons and silver weapons overcome this DR.

**Stain:** If you touch a good-aligned item, a *holy* weapon fusion, or a silver item, including being struck by a good-aligned or silver weapon, you are sickened for 1 round. Your immunities don't prevent this sickened condition, and you can't remove it early by any means. You can hide your aversion with a Bluff check opposed by Sense Motive checks.

## VELSTRAC REJUVENATION

You exist in a state between mortal and velstrac, placing you at risk of becoming a velstrac when you die.

**Prerequisites:** Pain Refuge, Painful Clarity, Velstrac Durability.

**Gift:** Twice per day, you can grant yourself fast healing 3 for 1 minute. Your fast healing functions only while you have 1 Hit Point or more.

**Stain:** Whenever you gain the dying condition, you lose 1 Resolve Point. In addition, it costs you 1 extra Resolve Point

(maximum of 4 instead of 3) to stabilize yourself. If you die, you have a 50% chance to reincarnate as an NPC velstrac (an outsider) on the Shadow Plane. If you do, you can be raised from the dead only via *miracle* or *wish* along with a soul beacon as if casting *raise dead* on an undead target.

## VOID HEART

The darkness in your soul can draw on the life force of allies.

**Prerequisites:** One other manifestation.

**Gift:** Once per day when you take ability damage, ability drain, or Hit Point damage, you can divide the damage or drain evenly between you and one ally within 30 feet of you. The ally knows what you're trying to do and can attempt a Will saving throw to resist the link. This ability takes no action on your part, and you can use it even if it isn't your turn.

**Stain:** You struggle to remember the meaning of friendly bonds. You can't benefit from or use the aid another action.

# OTHER CORRUPTIONS

Shadow corruption is one of many paranormal afflictions. Summaries of numerous other corruptions follow, suggesting possible manifestations and cures.

## ACCURSED

A foul curse from a supernatural creature, such as a vengeful spirit or cruel hag, imposes the accursed corruption, which amplifies the victim's hateful emotions. Even after the curse is lifted, this resentment lingers. The victim lashes out against perceived slights and grows ever more spiteful. As the corruption takes root, she can stagger enemies with a glare, turn them into harmless beasts, or slash them with claws that drain a foe's strength. She might even become powerful enough to twist the strands of fate or grant a twisted wish. However, she grows allergic to cold iron, balks at helping her allies, and takes on a horrific appearance with bulging, bloodshot eyes. Removing this corruption requires seeking the forgiveness of the one who cast the original curse and undoing any harm caused by using the corruption's gifts.

## GHOUL

Ghoul fever can transform a person into a ghoul after death, but ghoul corruption is subtler. It takes hold in someone who has withstood ghoul fever or in someone who has resorted to cannibalism. Unbidden, the urge to consume the flesh of a living or recently dead sentient creature surfaces within him. He might be able to restrain himself for short periods, but the sight of a fresh corpse tests his resolve. Manifestations include claws, fangs, and the stench of the grave. He might gain the ability to paralyze foes and to absorb the knowledge in a brain by eating it. The victim is also difficult to heal with magic and clumsy with manufactured weapons. Surviving this corruption requires an extended period of fasting and isolation, and perhaps a divine blessing.

## HELLBOUND

Some gain the hellbound corruption by making deals with the devils of Hell. Others carry this corruption due to infernal ancestry. The prospect of hellish eternity weighs on the victim until she gives in, fulfilling a prophecy of damnation. As the corruption takes root, she begins to resemble a devil. Dark tutors teach her the Infernal language, sinister persuasion methods, and other forbidden knowledge. She might be able to glimpse the future or teleport by stepping through Hell. The corruption slowly changes her into a lawful evil fiend, eventually making it impossible to raise her from the dead. Purging this corruption requires atoning for vile deeds, destroying fiendish contracts, and relinquishing rewards for them. Doing so might involve seeking the aid of a powerful celestial.

## LYCANTHROPY

When a character survives a lycanthrope attack, the lycanthropy corruption may ensue. This corruption turns the victim into a feral beast. The civilized world becomes a straitjacket, restraining him from tearing anyone he dislikes limb from limb. Lycanthropy manifestations include the ability to shift into a bestial form with enhanced strength and senses. Silver burns the victim's flesh, and he finds it hard to resist effects that manipulate his emotions. The victim blacks out and wakes up to evidence of carnage he has caused. Consuming doses of the poison belladonna and slaying the lycanthropy's source can alleviate this corruption.

## MUTANT

Whether from radiation or genetic engineering, the mutant corruption radically alters a victim's DNA. Her physical form transforms in ways that become more drastic over time. She could grow an extra limb, several more eyes, a prehensile tail, or anatomy that's more alien. Her skin might grow thinner or more susceptible to energy damage. Outward transformations accompany variations in personality. Perhaps the victim no longer sees herself as a member of her own species, grows to resent those not afflicted by mutations, or believes herself to be a superior evolutionary product. In any case, she feels out of touch with and could attempt to destroy non-mutants. The mutant corruption is akin to a disease and might be treatable with gene therapy and other medical procedures.

## NANITE

Nanites—microscopic robots that rearrange matter—can be a blessing, but their programming can become corrupted. A character who has nanite corruption has been injected with nanites that are out of control and slowly taking over his body. The nanites might have been intended to heal, but as their code degrades, they change the host instead. Benefits of nanite corruption include faster healing, various immunities, and the ability to use the nanites for attacks or defenses. However, the host loses emotions and begins to see the faults in organic life. Electricity can send his body into painful spasms. Being saved from nanite corruption requires the nearly impossible removal of all rogue nanites, followed by months of recovery.

## POSSESSED

The possessed corruption centers on a second mind vying to control the victim's body, although the source of that mind could be anything from a spirit to a personality brought about by psychological trauma. Regardless, the victim's allies notice small changes in her personality as the second mind exerts more influence. This corruption aids the victim against mental attacks and can grant her supernatural powers, but the second mind gains more control over her actions and could consider her friends to be strangers or worse. Ending this corruption involves casting out the second mind through methods such as exorcism, fulfilling a possessing spirit's unfinished business, or undergoing extensive therapy.

## VAMPIRISM

When a vampire has fed on a character but then lets the victim live, that target might contract the vampirism corruption. Referred to as vampire spawn, someone who has this corruption transforms into a vampire over time as her thirst for blood grows. She might start by feeding on small beasts, but soon she begins to crave the blood of sapient beings. She also sees herself as a superior creature free to treat lesser organisms as playthings and food. As she gives in to the corruption, she gains vampiric powers, such as supernatural allure, command of animals, and the ability to transform into a cloud of mist when severely wounded. Before long, she casts no reflection, can't stand direct sunlight, and can enter private residences only after being invited. Slaying the original vampire and forsaking blood are essential to ending this corruption, along with magical purification.

## VOID

Someone who ponders too long the vast emptiness of space or the destructive forces therein risks contracting void corruption. Devotion to the Devourer is a possible avenue to this corruption and a path to becoming an atrocite (*Starfinder Adventure Path #4* 56). Perhaps dark meditation opens the mind to nihilistic entities that live in the darkest reaches of the planes. The corrupted character has nightmares in which an apocalyptic catastrophe or unfathomable being consumes all life. Eventually, these visions bleed into the waking state. The victim learns to temporarily befuddle others' perceptions and to summon creatures from the void. However, his own awareness is altered and physical mutations mark him as a servant of nullity. Only a grounding connection to loved ones and therapy that rights the void-wrought changes can bring the victim back.

# HORROR CAMPAIGNS

"We're the first genre, gifted to our ancestors in their primordial nightmares. We're a warning against savage mortality lurking in a cramped, cruel universe. All other genres stand in opposition to us—heroes slaying dragons, lovers stealing kisses, detectives uncovering injustices. They're distractions invented to hold back the darkness, to dull life's bloody edges with hope and familiarity.

"But the cosmos is darkness. We were the first, and when entropy comes in its myriad forms—a great slavering maw, an alien pathogen, or a sinister secret behind a neighbor's smile—on that day we will also be the last."

—Abri Anned, famed Vercite horror director and philanthropist

Starfinder is already a wondrous collection of genres—star pilots, scoundrels, freebooters, and mystics hopping from alien world to alien world in search of adventure and glory. Science fiction, fantasy, and good old-fashioned action collide in a perilous universe. In all this space, there's plenty of room for at least one more genre. Rejoice!

Or, perhaps, despair. For in the lightless void between the stars lurks an older and darkly fascinating wonder: horror. It's an oft-misunderstood genre that is, by itself, a complex cosmos encompassing a variety of flavors, tones, and subgenres.

That's why horror is a hard genre to define. Only some horror is frightening, and something scary might fail to be horror. Some horror relies on tension and jump scares to start your heart racing. Other horror methodically slips in dreadful clues to freeze your blood when their true meaning is revealed. Some horror throws heroes into the thresher only to watch them emerge brutalized but triumphant. Other horror never lets its protagonists up for air, leaving its audience traumatized. Some horror drives a stake deep into the heart of our cultural flaws. Other horror plays its tropes for laughs.

The ancient tree of horror drinks the first fears of our ancestors in through its roots and stretches its branches into an endless night in search of new genres that are emerging from the darkness. These pages contain tools to help you and your fellow players seek out what brought you to this genre. Further, you'll find tools to help you define horror—not to delineate the genre, but to find the sort of horror you want in your game.

## TYPES OF HORROR

Listed hereafter is a selection of horror subgenres that meld well with other Starfinder genres. As you prepare to play a horror campaign, discuss the characters' role within the subgenres you're considering. Establish whether the PCs are potential victims of the horror, its witnesses, or both.

### ACTION HORROR

Starfinder is about action heroes braving challenges others are unwilling to face. Action horror is about that, but with a menace that is just as relentless as the heroes, whether it's hordes of undead or one monstrous alien crawling through the ventilation system of a starship. This sort of horror pits the protagonists against a problem they might not be able to confront with their usual methods. Even if those techniques are effective, they might not be reliable or they could produce unexpected results.

Witnesses of action horror discover this unrelenting threat when it plagues someone else, perhaps those close to the heroes. Such a situation plays out like a normal Starfinder game, but with dreadful stakes. Victims of action horror know or learn that standing and fighting is a last resort—far better to run, find safety, regroup, and attack only when conditions are at their most desperate or when the moment is just right.

### BODY HORROR

At its heart, body horror is about physiology behaving in unnatural ways, betraying its owner's expectations and sense of self. Starfinder is filled with aliens and other creatures that have unusual forms. These facts provide ample opportunity to introduce body horror, but they can also lessen its impact. When any character can have a body that behaves as human and insect, lizard, or rat, it can be hard to find the terror in a misplaced limb or waking up with a new mouth growing on your arm.

The key is to anchor body horror in the mundane. Witnessing body horror means interacting with creepy monsters that begin as normal individuals but whose bodies behave in troubling ways. Victims of body horror might suffer according to the affliction rules (*Starfinder Core Rulebook* 414), the phantasm rules in "The Diaspora Strain" (see page 20), and the "Corrupted by Shadows" article in this book (see pages 40–45). All of these can be used to sever the bond of trust between PCs and their bodies.

### COSMIC HORROR

The stars have aligned and awoken a being older than time whose very existence renders our own moot. Cosmic horror relies on the existential fear that we aren't the most significant creatures in the universe. Instead, some horrific intelligence from eons past holds dominion over the cosmos. This subgenre pairs well with others, since the true nature of the universe is in question.

Witnesses of cosmic horror might be able to do something about it. They look upon this terror and despair no more than when they face any other titanic fiend and its worshipers. Victims of cosmic horror are forced into despair that their world is not what it seems. They tangle with cultists and lesser monsters, but faced with the true menace, corruption and afflictions turn their world upside down.

### PSYCHOLOGICAL HORROR

Characters in a psychological horror story are victims of their own anxiety, belief, doubt, guilt, and passion. Psychological horror is rooted in the personal. It can manifest internally, driving a character to self-destructive or appalling action. If this horror occurs externally, a character's troubles could take phantasmal form or manifest as a monster.

Witnesses of psychological horror encounter NPCs with unnatural or troubling behaviors. Each one's psyche compels them to do the shocking and unthinkable. Victims can find themselves facing a creature, phantasmal or real, that mirrors their own fears or guilt. Alternatively, they might instead struggle internally with a curse-like affliction using the normal Starfinder rules.

## PREPARING FOR HORROR

We must ask ourselves what draws us here. What do we seek in the macabre, unsettling, and repulsive realms of horror? What is so fascinating and thrilling about such a morbid genre?

Answers to these questions are neither easy nor unanimous. As you delve together into this abyss, you could find that you and your fellow players disagree.

Before you play in any type of horror game, examine the following questions as a group, including the GM.

- Why horror? What compels us to play a horror game?
- What's out? What do we leave unexplored?
- What's scary? Within the bounds we've established, what scares us the most?

The following sections examine each of these questions in more detail. But first, a word of caution:

*Don't judge your fellow players.*

Everyone, player and GM alike, should answer these questions as honestly as possible. Don't feel you need to be brave or that your answers should be edgy. You might find sexy vampires the most compelling horror, leaving all else unexplored. The scariest thought could be that such a vampire might not love you. These are legitimate answers.

Likewise, don't conceal the horror fan that lurks inside you. Be respectful of your fellow players, and spare them unsettling or shocking details. However, if you're fascinated by tales of forced surgery, wish to leave nothing unexplored, and can think of little more terrifying than self-inflicted violence on your own eyes, this is the genre for you.

To find the boundaries for your group, start safe and probe outward. Ask in vague terms if its okay for you to describe violence before going on to depict it. If someone says no, stop there and go no further—they don't need to explain. You have found a boundary. Make note of it. Do not cross it.

Together, you explore horror with careful attention paid to each other's limits and comfort. You shouldn't judge each other for what you each find scary or for what you each find fascinating. You accept and work within the affordances and constraints you build together. Chase thrills together, but keep each other safe.

## WHY HORROR?

Take turns naming one thing you find compelling about playing a horror game. Is it a fear you want to face? A monster you'd like to confront? A feeling? A specific scenario? What horror media have you enjoyed?

Heed your fellow players' answers. Respond to them. Does the same thing compel you? Is it something you're willing to explore? And if it is, does it give you any ideas about what shared interests you can explore together?

You need your players' consent for a horror game. If someone in your group isn't uncomfortable playing in a horror game, set it aside as a genre—there are many other great options available!

## WHAT'S OUT?

It's likely you already have some answers to this question based on the previous one. That's as it should be. Here we find the boundaries of play. If there are places you don't want to go in a horror game, bring them up. You needn't explain why. You need only tell your fellow players where those boundaries are.

During this question, you might acknowledge, agree with, or ask for clarification from your fellow players. However, don't justify why you want to explore a horror element someone else is unwilling to delve into, and never argue or push back. Enforce your pact. None shall be judged—neither them for their aversion, nor you for your interest.

## WHAT'S SCARY?

Now, consider what has already been discussed and take turns finding what scares you. Players each offer horror elements they find to be scary, revealing something that terrifies them but exists within the boundaries you already established as a group.

This frightening thing doesn't have to be specific to the Starfinder universe. It doesn't need to be original, either. It could be a movie you saw, a book you read, another game you played, or a nightmare you've had.

Reasons for this exploration are twofold. First, you might find someone's answer to this question crossing a line you didn't know you had. Speak up, and as before, say only that you wish to leave the subject unexplored. No justification is needed. If someone stops you while you give your answer, be respectful of their boundary and find a new answer. You needn't justify your answer. Second, this discussion sets the mood and whets your appetites. It lets you prepare for the horrors that lie ahead.

## PLAYING HORROR GAMES

A horror roleplaying game is not a horror movie or a novel. Differences among mediums warrant special attention. Chief among these are the players and their characters.

When you consume horror media, you can envision yourself in the characters' place and sympathize with their plight. You can feel terror through them. Or, you can distance yourself by insisting you'd never make the mistakes they're making, never fall for the traps they fall for, and never behave as selfishly or repugnantly as they do. You can even make this decision unconsciously as someone's fate changes during the tale.

As you play a horror game, however, you are responsible for your character's actions, thoughts, and behavior. Since you are the creator of these aspects of your character, you can't make unconscious decisions about how you relate to them. You must make conscious ones.

Before you play, answer the following questions about how you prefer to play. Keep these issues in mind as you play, as well.

- Who's afraid? Is it the player, the character, or both?
- Who's the focus? Are PCs witnesses, victims, or both?
- How can you opt out? If you find a boundary you didn't expect, how can you retreat back across it?

## WHO'S AFRAID?

When playing, whose fears are you addressing? They could be your fears or your character's. The two can align, but in many cases, they won't.

If you wish to be scared, help the GM out. Offer up fears you're willing to face. Place your character in situations where these fears must be confronted. Be honest about your reactions to these fears, even if they aren't your character's. Accept the disadvantages that might occur in the game due to the horror.

Many reasons exist why someone might want to feel frightened, including the desire to witness someone overcome that fear. This form of pretending can be very effective if you play a character who doesn't share your fears, who wanders into a dark room despite your grave misgivings. Similarly, you might wish to revel in your terror and play a character with the same fears, who flees when you would, intent on staying whole and safe.

If you want only your character to be scared, help the GM and the other players out. Offer up the PC's fears and play to them when they show up in the game. How does your character react? The way a character reacts to a fearful situation might be contrary to what folks would expect in a typical Starfinder game. Make sure your fellow players know when a decision is your character's decision and not yours. As your party plans the next move, your frightened character might argue against actions that you, as a player, think are strategically or narratively favorable. You can work with your fellow players to find a way to convince your character, or the group might agree to let your character make a dangerous or unhelpful choice.

## WHO'S THE FOCUS?

It's also important to consider, with the GM, whether the PCs are to be witnesses of horrors affecting those around them or they are themselves the victims of that horror. They could also move between these roles, which is usual in most horror stories.

Starfinder PCs are ready-made to be witnesses to someone else's horror story. They can step in and apply their ample will and might to the situation. If you can adjust your expectations to such circumstances, it's still possible to have creepy and unsettling adventures. Odds are, the PCs are unlikely to remain passive witnesses for long, but the shift in focus can be on your terms.

If you chose for your PCs to be potential victims, expectations must again be adjusted. Your character might not remain a passive victim for long, but you should spend some time relishing the terror. Embrace the fear, even if it comes with mechanical disadvantages in the game.

Find small victories, and steel yourself for what's to come. When your PC is a victim, elements that might seem unfair or unbalanced, especially in a non-horror context, can instead serve to create the horror.

## OPTING OUT

Despite your careful planning and setting of boundaries for your horror game, you might run into a situation in which a limit is reached, whether known or previously unknown—no one can be expected to realize all their boundaries before the game. Therefore, it is vital that players are free to end a game situation that's too much for them at any time, without having to explain and without questions or judgment from fellow players or the GM.

Before beginning play, agree on a way to allow someone to opt out as quickly and wordlessly as possible. Quickly, so the game doesn't continue to cross a boundary, and wordlessly, so no explanation needs to be given. Each player, including the GM, might have a token they can hold up to silently indicate opting out.

When a player opts out, stop what's happening in the game immediately. If you, as a GM, need clarification on what needs to change before the game can continue, take the player aside and talk. This conversation takes place only so you can understand what bothered the player and what the boundary is. The player doesn't need to explain why they feel the way they do. After clarification, as with other limits agreed upon for the game, don't cross that boundary again.

## RUNNING HORROR GAMES

The challenge for any GM of a horror game is to take a game about brave adventurers who launch themselves into the void in search of the unknown and bring the stark terror of their reality to the forefront. This task isn't easy, but you don't have to do it alone. Recruit the players as your allies. Reach out to them, encourage them, and check in with them. Find out how they're doing and how they feel you're doing. Make sure that no one's limits have been crossed.

If your goal is to scare the players, rather than just their characters, you need their consent and their buy-in. They can tell you what scares them and what their boundaries are. Listen to them. Ask them whether they're willing to buy in, and help them do so if they are.

Don't forget to scare yourself, too. Terror in a horror game shouldn't be a one-way street. Answer the pre-game questions with the players. Find what fascinates you about the genre and what you want to explore. Share with your players before you play. Anticipation of exploring what was revealed in those exercises only serves to build tension.

If you, as a group, have decided that the characters are to be scared rather than the players, you still have plenty of horror tools, tropes, and themes at your disposal.

Here are some options that can help you build a horror experience tailored to your group.

## PERSONAL AND IMPERSONAL

When creating a menace to terrorize the PCs, the personal is scarier than the impersonal. Focus on something hooked into the story of the PCs or their players, whichever you've agreed to scare. Set your sights on fears brought up in the discussion with your players. Invest some time in pondering those fears, finding your menace in the metaphor. The following examples can guide you in exploring other fears.

**Animals:** Many folks are willing to explore a fear of animals, such as wild dogs, spiders, or sharks. But what is it about these animals that might cause fear? You can offer monstrous or alien versions of animals, but dig into why such a fear might exist. Are wild dogs scary because they're feral versions of beloved pets? What do the PCs cherish that you can twist into a feral version? Are spiders fearsome because of the way they move or because they could be lurking anywhere? Are sharks terrifying because they move about unseen and strike from the depths? How can you tap these fears?

**Infection:** Hordes of undead, a lycanthrope's bite, a world-spanning pandemic—so much horror has been drawn from the festering well of infection. The affliction rules in Starfinder and the corruption rules in this book cover what happens once you're infected. However, it's up to you to uncover the nature of the fear. Does it originate in vulnerability to the unseen? Is it a fear of losing agency over body or health? Could it be an apocalyptic fear about the fate of civilization? Or is it born of a deeper fear of losing your sense of self once you've been infected?

**Invasion:** Horror and science fiction genres overlap with tales of alien invasions. These incursions can take numerous forms, including military and technological might that hammers society to the ground, insidious infiltration through shapeshifting or mental domination, harvesters and butchers disguised as ambassadors, or beings from between galaxies that treat other species as trivial. Dig into the fears that can manifest in these tales. Is loss of cultural identity terrifying? Could it be a primal fear of becoming prey? Is it the terror that familiar people could turn against you?

## REAL AND UNREAL

The balance between the real and the unreal is important in a horror story. So is the power to switch between the two.

Unreal elements allow us to distance ourselves from horror. The unreal not only can produce wonder and awe, which are akin to horror, but can also offer reprieve. Imagine the following scene.

---

A giant pillar composed of fleshy faces twists as it towers over a barren plain. Twin suns set behind it.

---

That scene isn't comforting, but it's also unreal. Players can, therefore, hold it at a distance. If there's too much unreality, that distance grows, overwhelming horror with mere spectacle. However, the mundane anchors us, even if its something real twisted to fit the horror. Imagine if the previous scene were presented the following way.

---

Your companion leans forward and takes tentative steps toward the pillar, his head cocked. He looks back, brow furrowed, and says, "Don't you hear it? They're whispering our names."

---

As you prepare horror adventures, keep this balance in mind. Think about where you want to emphasize the unreal and where you want to nail the real. This tool can also shine in play. When you're running your game and find you need to shake things up, ask yourself, is this situation or scene more unreal or more real? Then look for a way to push the narrative in the opposite direction.

## REASON AND PERCEPTION

The Starfinder universe is filled with strange beings, alien cultures, and unfamiliar ways of thinking. The PCs rely on reason and perception to take in all of this possibility and parse it into motivations and actions. Taking the PCs and shaking them from this paradigm into one that repulses or frightens them can make for compelling material. PCs unable to trust their senses or how those senses are interpreted in the mind can suffer intense anxiety. Having perceptions rewired by a drug, an experience, or a word can be truly terrifying, especially when the menace hides just beneath those alterations or in plain sight among false sensory input.

These grounds are fruitful for a horror game, and you can explore them to great effect without resorting to stigmatizing and stereotyping mental illness. Don't talk about PCs losing their sanity. Focus instead on the shift in their perceptions and their way of thinking. Emphasize what's actually happening to them.

In many cases, such as with the phantasm rules in this adventure, you'll be describing things to players that their characters experience, but those situations won't be accurate. Although it isn't necessary to forewarn players about exact circumstances, it is important that they understand they're partaking in situations where all is not as it seems. Some truths might be hidden, and some falsehoods might seem true. Horrible secrets might be kept from them until the right moment. All these obfuscations might have hidden mechanical effects in the game. Knowing these possibilities ahead of time allows players to prepare for disagreeable surprises that could seem unfair without this context.

## UNKNOWN AND KNOWN

Tension is a part of every adventure, horror or not, and it is most often found at that moment just before a critical roll—before the unknown becomes known. The task before you is not to create tension so much as draw it out. You want to sow doubt, causing growing anxiety over the outcome. This is a balancing act between hope and despair. Shift too far either way, and no doubt remains.

You can use the unknown and the known as tools in this vein. This tactic works much like using the real and the unreal in equal measures.

**Unknown:** The truth behind the horror is hidden, unknown, the mystery to be solved. Not every horror story needs a mystery, but mystery is a classic way to build tension. Hide the true menace. Show the aftermath, like so:

---

Globules of blood and viscera float in microgravity. Everything else in the airlock is pristine.

---

Or, show the prelude like so:

---

The countless people on the city streets stop. As a unit, they turn to stare at the same distant point. An inhuman scream from that direction hits like thunder. Then, the people start to walk toward it.

---

The cause remains indiscernible in either case.

Because the cause is unclear, you can reveal that cause slowly. Let the PCs chase after it, uncover clues, find red herrings, and develop theories. Don't place your true menace in a position where it can be forced into a confrontation sooner than you want.

**Known:** Great tension can be found in the known. The known is horrifying when the truth is plain, and it doesn't look good. It might look something like this:

---

Down the tunnel, deeper into the asteroid mine, other survivors huddle at their own barricade. A few infected creep into the intersection between their barrier and yours. Then more come, and more… and more.

---

In this case, the players know what's at stake. Show them the ghastly challenge before them. Prepare them for a Pyrrhic victory. Often this sort of tension hinges on the fact that the PCs can't save everyone. They might even have to decide who to save, and who to leave behind to a known and horrendous fate.

## ISOLATION AND BETRAYAL

A common theme in horror is the loss of social safeguards. This situation happens because lines of communication and routes to safety are cut off. It also happens when those who maintain safety act inappropriately. Is the real danger the unknown pathogen loose in the colony, or the doctor who's secretly infecting colonists with it for further tests?

Starfinder PCs don't rely on authority figures often, but in a horror game, it's important to hold even these rare appeals to authority at bay. When preparing your game, find ways to ensure authorities can't be reached, are less effective in response to the menace than the PCs, or have an agenda or problem that makes them as dangerous as—or even part of—the menace. For example, Stewards might arrive in good faith to help fight the mind-controlling alien symbiotes, only for each to quickly fall victim to the invaders because one of them was already under the symbiotes' control.

## DEATH AND REBIRTH

Death is more common in horror games than in typical Starfinder games. How you plan to deal with this aspect of horror needs to be clear from the start. You and your players should set expectations before play. Everyone needs to understand how likely PC death is and how it will be treated. Some forewarning helps your players buy in.

If a PC dies, normal methods for bringing back the dead are an option. However, the intersection of science fantasy and horror offers other options, including weird science, sinister sorceries, dark pacts, and spontaneous reanimation (as with borais; *Pact Worlds* 211). Only a couple questions need to be answered. What ghastly options do PCs have for revivification? What horrific price do they have to pay to use those options?

## PLAYER OPTIONS

The following player options help support a horror theme.

### FEATS

These horror-based feats focus on accepting weaknesses or shoring them up.

#### CRAVEN PLOY (COMBAT)

When the going gets tough, you hide behind allies.

**Prerequisites:** Cha 13.

**Benefit:** As a reaction when you are attacked while adjacent to an ally, if that ally is willing to take a –2 penalty to her Armor Class until the beginning of her next turn, you gain a +2 circumstance bonus to your AC against that attack.

#### INDIRECT RETREAT (COMBAT)

You can run through winding corridors and weave your way through grasping claws without pause.

**Prerequisites:** Dex 13, Mobility.

**Benefit:** When you run as a full action, you don't have to move in a straight line, you can run across difficult terrain, and you don't gain the flat-footed condition.

#### STARTLED SCREAM

When something bad is about to go down, you scream to let everyone know.

**Benefit:** Before initiative is rolled during an encounter, you can scream as part of combat banter (*Core Rulebook* 249) even if you're surprised. If you do, allies who are surprised but can hear you don't gain the flat-footed condition, while allies who aren't surprised gain a +1 insight bonus to initiative checks. You gain the appropriate benefit depending on whether you are surprised or not. However, your scream is loud, possibly drawing the attention of foes that can hear you and alerting others within earshot. You're also shaken until the end of your next turn.

#### STEEL NERVES

You retain your reason when you're scared.

**Prerequisites:** Wis 13, character level 3rd.

**Benefit:** You gain a +2 bonus to saving throws against fear effects. In addition, when you have the frightened condition, you can choose to fight rather than flee. When you have the panicked condition, you don't drop what you're holding.

#### WARY WITHDRAWAL (COMBAT)

You know how to withdraw with great caution.

**Prerequisites:** Dex 13, Wis 13, Mobility.

**Benefit:** When you use the total defense action, you can also withdraw as a move action. If you do so, you can move only up to your speed.

### SPELLS

The following spells have a horror theme. The cantor velstrac also uses them (see page 60).

## NIGHTMARE

**School** illusion (mind-affecting)
**Casting Time** 10 minutes
**Range** plane
**Targets** one living creature
**Duration** instantaneous
**Saving Throw** Will negates; **Spell Resistance** yes

You precisely identify a target, such as by name or via a material connection like a personal possession or lock of its hair. The spell fails without expending a spell slot if the target isn't asleep or in a resting state similar to sleep. If you've never met the target in person and lack a material connection to the target, the target gains a +5 bonus to the saving throw. If the spell works, the target remains resting for 1 minute, then has a nightmare, rouses, and becomes frightened for 2d6 rounds. The target can't willingly reenter the affected resting state for 1 hour. To do so after this time has elapsed, the target must succeed at the saving throw again. If this save fails, the target can try again once per hour thereafter. After 24 hours have passed, this restless state ends.

## PARANOIA

**School** illusion (mind-affecting)
**Casting Time** 1 standard action
**Range** close (25 ft. + 5 ft./2 levels)
**Targets** one creature
**Duration** 1 round/level (D)
**Saving Throw** Will negates; **Spell Resistance** yes

The target treats all other creatures as enemies and only itself as an ally. It must attempt attacks of opportunity whenever any creature provokes them. In addition, the target is shaken while adjacent to more than one creature.

## SHADOW BODY

**School** transmutation (polymorph, shadow)
**Casting Time** 1 standard action
**Range** personal
**Duration** 1 minute/level (D)

You transform the matter of your body and any objects you carry or wear into the essence of the Shadow Plane. You are visible as an unattached shadow in bright light or normal light, but you gain total concealment in dim light or darkness (reduced to concealment against creatures that have darkvision). Your body and gear are incorporeal, but you can't fly or pass through solid objects or creatures, and your gear can't be removed from you or used by anyone. You can move at your normal speed along any surface, including horizontal and vertical surfaces and liquids, and difficult terrain doesn't slow you. However, you can't attack physically or manipulate objects. You can speak, cast spells that require no items to cast, and perform mental actions. If you can use spells that have a range of touch and such a spell requires an attack roll, you target EAC. If you lose consciousness, you and your gear return to your natural form.

# PARANORMAL INVESTIGATOR  +1 INT, WIS OR CHA

Some, upon waking, want to forget their nightmares, find comfort among their companions, and dream of new adventures. That's not you. No, you know waking life can be a dream and the nightmares can be real. You are a truth-seeker, chasing the shadows in search of a world hidden behind the veneer of normalcy. Each fresh horror you uncover proves your work is right and important, and makes you want to delve deeper into the galaxy's haunting secrets.

## THEME KNOWLEDGE (1ST)

You're skilled at identifying patterns, finding clues, and piecing together puzzles about the paranormal. No two investigators do so in the same way. Choose Diplomacy, Life Science, Mysticism, Physical Science, or Survival. The chosen skill is a class skill for you, and it's your field for other theme features. If the chosen skill is a class skill from the class you take at 1st level, you instead gain a +1 bonus to checks with it. In addition, at character creation, you gain an ability adjustment of +1 to the ability score associated with your chosen skill.

You choose a specific paranormal mystery case that you and the GM create. Reduce the DCs of checks to recall knowledge about and gather information related to your case by 5. You can similarly reduce the DCs of checks to recall knowledge about notable personalities, practices, and events in the paranormal realm and your field. After solving a case, you can take on another after 1 day of studying evidence for a new case. You can abandon a case without solving it to take on a new one. If you do so, you take a –2 penalty to skill checks for 1 week.

## ATTENTION TO DETAIL (6TH)

Halve the time it takes you to gather information (minimum 30 minutes), search an area, or perform research to take 20 when recalling knowledge or identifying a creature, a magic item, or technology. In addition, once per day, if you fail a Perception or Sense Motive check or a check in your field, you can reroll the check and use the higher result.

## GNAWING HUNCH (12TH)

You've learned to trust your hunches. If a clue can be found by taking 20 on a Perception check or a skill check in your field, the GM must tell you such a clue exists, but not what it is. Once you know a clue exists, you just have to find it.

## TRUTH-SEEKER (18TH)

Organizing evidence about your case and researching it refreshes you and sets you back on your path. Twice per day, you can take 10 minutes to consider and record your findings or look for new insights into them. If you do so,

you regain 1 Resolve Point and can recall knowledge. If you instead take 1 hour, you regain 1 Resolve Point and can gather information. Neither of these tasks count as resting to regain Stamina Points.

# ALIEN ARCHIVES

"Look, people disappear in my establishment. It happens. Not often enough to hurt my business, but it's a fact of life out here in the Armada. Plenty of reasons, too. Bad luck, bad blood, and, you know, occasional undesirable elements. Hells, I even heard there's this critter from the Vast that lives in shipping crates. Eats dockworkers. Like they don't have it bad enough. But, hey, I get it. Someone goes missing here, and you come knocking on my door. That's fine. I got nothing for you, but at least I ain't insulted, right? Now, I think we're done. Don't let the airlock clip you on the way out."

—King Curney, on disappearances at
King Curney's Kasbah

# CRATE FIEND

N Medium vermin

**Init** +2; **Senses** blindsense (vibration) 60 ft., darkvision 60 ft.; Perception +8

**DEFENSE**      **HP** 30

**EAC** 15; **KAC** 17

**Fort** +7; **Ref** +5; **Will** +2

**Defensive Abilities** crate shell; **Resistances** acid 5

**OFFENSE**

**Speed** 20 ft. (40 ft. outside crate shell)

**Melee** bite +11 (1d6+7 A & P; critical corrode 1d4) or claw +11 (1d6+7 S and grab)

**Ranged** acid blast +9 (explode [5 ft., 1d6+1 A plus 1d4 corrode, DC 12])

**Offensive Abilities** explosive death

**STATISTICS**

**Str** +2; **Dex** +1; **Con** +4; **Int** —; **Wis** +0; **Cha** –3

**Skills** Athletics +8, Stealth +13

**Other Abilities** compression, mindless

**ECOLOGY**

**Environment** any urban or land (Taekah III)

**Organization** solitary, pair, or rack (3–5)

**SPECIAL ABILITIES**

**Acid Blast (Ex)** As a standard action, a crate fiend can launch an acid blast with a range increment of 20 feet.

**Crate Shell (Ex)** A crate fiend dwells within a container as if it were the creature's shell. While inside its container and motionless, a crate fiend appears to be the container. As a move action, a crate fiend can partially or fully withdraw into its shell. If it partially withdraws, it gains partial cover but takes a –2 penalty to attack rolls and can move at only half speed. While fully withdrawn, the fiend can neither move nor attack but has total cover. The container has AC 10, hardness 10, and 22 Hit Points. The fiend has a –2 penalty to AC in a container that has the broken condition. If the container is destroyed, the penalty increases to –4. A crate fiend can adapt to a new container in 1 hour.

**Explosive Death (Ex)** When a crate fiend dies, as no action on its part, it makes an acid blast attack. The attack's point of origin must be adjacent to the creature's space.

Crate fiends, properly called taekahbs, are bizarre arthropods that originated on Taekah III, a habitable world in the Vast. On this planet, these soft-shelled scavengers seek homes in the cast-off shells of larger native gastropods or nodules of volcanic pumice the taekahbs hollow out with their acid. Crate fiends breed quickly, laying hidden caches of eggs that are scented so other crate fiends find and fertilize them.

When they migrated offworld, no doubt due to careless smugglers or foolish zoologists, crate fiends found homes in the maintenance tunnels and ventilation systems of starships and space stations, as well as in the nooks and crannies of industrialized settlements. Discarded shipping containers proved to be fine homes for them, earning the taekahbs their common name, since they can use such abodes to hide in plain sight. These beasts prefer to eat refuse and carrion, and they avoid discovery and confrontation. However, larger crate fiends have been known to kill and consume dockworkers and unlucky passersby.

# GLOOMWING

**CR 4**
**XP 1,200**

N Large outsider (extraplanar)
**Init** +5; **Senses** darkvision 60 ft.; **Perception** +10

## DEFENSE
**HP** 50
**EAC** 16; **KAC** 18
**Fort** +6; **Ref** +8; **Will** +3

## OFFENSE
**Speed** 10 ft., fly 40 ft. (Ex, average)
**Melee** bite +13 (1d6+6 P)
**Space** 10 ft.; **Reach** 5 ft.
**Offensive Abilities** confusion, implant, pheromones

## STATISTICS
**Str** +2; **Dex** +5; **Con** +2; **Int** –4; **Wis** +0; **Cha** +0
**Skills** Acrobatics +15, Stealth +10

## ECOLOGY
**Environment** any land or sky (Shadow Plane)
**Organization** solitary or pair

## SPECIAL ABILITIES
**Confusion (Su)** The shifting patterns on a gloomwing's wings are hypnotic. A creature that starts its turn able to see the gloomwing must succeed at a DC 13 Will saving throw or become confused for 1 round. A creature can avoid looking directly at the gloomwing to gain a +4 bonus to the saving throw. However, doing so causes the creature to treat the gloomwing as if it has concealment (20% miss chance). Gloomwings and tenebrous worms are immune to this effect. This is a mind-affecting, sense-dependent effect.

**Implant (Su)** As a full action, a gloomwing can lay eggs in a Small or larger helpless living creature. The target creature contracts tenebrous gestation (see below).

**Pheromones (Su)** Starting on the round after a gloomwing becomes agitated (typically the second round of combat), the creature exudes an invisible cloud of weakening pheromones that creates a musky scent. Living creatures other than gloomwings and tenebrous worms within this 30-foot aura must succeed at a DC 13 Fortitude saving throw or become fatigued for 1 hour.

## TENEBROUS GESTATION
**Type** disease (injury); **Save** Fortitude DC 13
**Track** physical (special);
**Frequency** 1/day
**Effect** no latent state; if the victim dies, 1d4 young tenebrous worms emerge 4d6 hours later and devour the corpse completely.
**Cure** 2 consecutive saves; the eggs can also be removed with a successful DC 13 Medicine check that takes 1 hour or if the victim is targeted by *remove affliction*.

Gloomwings are mothlike predators native to the Shadow Plane known to slip through the barrier with the Material Plane in places where the barrier is thin. Their bizarrely patterned wings can cause confusion in onlookers, even within the dimly lit, shadowy places where they rest. Gloomwings also have a distinct, musky scent. If a gloomwing becomes stressed, it releases its pheromone-laden musk, causing lethargy in other living creatures. The scent also attracts other gloomwings and their larvae, known as tenebrous worms (see page 59).

The chitin on a gloomwing's mandibles and head has a pearlescent quality, especially in normal and bright light. Some jewelers and mystics value this material. With a successful DC 21 Survival check that takes 10 minutes, a character can harvest 1d4 pieces of chitin, each worth 500 credits.

# REKLAN

N Small magical beast

**Init** +5; **Senses** blindsense (thought) 120 ft., darkvision 60 ft., low-light vision; **Perception** +14

**DEFENSE**   HP 110

**EAC** 19; **KAC** 21

**Fort** +9; **Ref** +11; **Will** +7

**OFFENSE**

**Speed** 40 ft., climb 40 ft., fly 40 ft. (Su, average), swim 40 ft.

**Melee** spiny tentacle +18 (2d8+7 P) or

bite +18 (2d6+11 P)

**Ranged** spine barrage +18 (2d8+7 P)

**STATISTICS**

**Str** +4; **Dex** +5; **Con** +2; **Int** –3; **Wis** +1; **Cha** +0

**Skills** Acrobatics +14, Athletics +14 (+22 to climb or swim), Stealth +19

**Other Abilities** compression, habitable field

**ECOLOGY**

**Environment** any (Diaspora)

**Organization** solitary or mating knot (2–7)

**SPECIAL ABILITIES**

**Habitable Field (Su)** A reklan generates a magical field that makes its surroundings habitable. This field extends in a spherical spread 1,200 feet from the reklan. Within this field, the reklan and other creatures are affected as if by the *life bubble* spell.

**Spine Barrage (Ex)** A reklan can fling its tail spines with a range increment of 60 feet.

Reklans are the result of an ancient sarcesian attempt to make the Diaspora more habitable through magical engineering. In one sense, the attempt succeeded—each reklan can magically provide a habitat comfortable to most Pact Worlds species in otherwise lifeless conditions. However, reklans turned on their creators. A reklan that senses a nearby sapient being immediately begins hunting it, stopping only when seriously wounded or killed, or when the intruder has been devoured.

Each reklan has two long, tentacular tails studded with bony spines similar to the creature's teeth. The reklan usually keeps these tails rolled up, but in combat, it lashes out with them, flicking detachable spines like darts. A reklan also has two sets of smaller front tentacles linked by webs of skin, which it flaps like wings. These tentacles attach just behind the reklan's fanged mouth. A typical reklan is only 3 feet long with its tails coiled. Most weigh around 90 pounds, and their spongy flesh allows them to squeeze through tiny spaces.

Reklans are native to the Diaspora, where they inhabit ruins they keep empty with their own hunting. They can also fly through vacuum in their magical bubbles. These creatures are usually found alone, although—because each reklan is capable of producing eggs and fertilizing the eggs of other reklans—they occasionally gather in small groups to mate.

Over the centuries, reklans have spread throughout the Pact Worlds and beyond, thanks to starfarers who use them as portable life-support systems. If kept carefully contained and unable to sense thought, a reklan is content to hibernate indefinitely, allowing captors to harness the beast's aura. Such arrangements are dangerous, though, since a reklan that breaks containment inevitably stalks its captors, stealthily moving through ventilation shafts and behind bulkheads to slaughter its prey with cunning efficiency.

**CR 9**    **XP 6,400**

N Large construct (technological)

**Init** +4; **Senses** darkvision 60 ft., low-light vision; Perception +17

## DEFENSE     HP 145

**EAC** 20; **KAC** 22

**Fort** +10; **Ref** +8; **Will** +6

**Defensive Abilities** integrated weapons, nanite repair; **Immunities** construct immunities; **Resistances** acid 5, fire 10

**Weaknesses** vulnerable to critical hits, vulnerable to electricity

## OFFENSE

**Speed** 30 ft., burrow 10 ft.

**Melee** drill +20 (3d4+14 P; critical bleed 2d4) or integrated andesite magma blade +20 (2d8+15 F & S; critical wound [DC 16])

**Ranged** integrated LFD screamer +17 (2d10+9 So; critical deafen [DC 16])

**Space** 10 ft.; **Reach** 10 ft.

## STATISTICS

**Str** +6; **Dex** +4; **Con** —; **Int** -2; **Wis** +3; **Cha** -3

**Skills** Profession (miner) +17

**Languages** Common (can't speak)

**Other Abilities** rock tunneler, unliving

**Gear** andesite magma blade^AR with 3 high-capacity batteries (40 charges each), LFD screamer with 2 super-capacity batteries (80 charges each)

## ECOLOGY

**Environment** any underground

**Organization** solitary, pair, or shift (3–5)

## SPECIAL ABILITIES

**Nanite Repair (Ex)** A mining robot's nanites heal it, restoring a number of Hit Points per hour equal to its CR (9 Hit Points per hour for most mining robots). Once per day as a full action, a mining robot can restore 4d8 Hit Points to itself or any touched construct with the technological subtype.

**Rock Tunneler (Ex)** A mining robot can burrow through stone at half speed, and it can choose to leave tunnels when it burrows.

Mining robots are far from exotic, but neither are they common since they are expensive tools. Such automatons allow mining companies to harvest ore and minerals from dangerous locales, such as airless asteroids and planets with high tectonic activity. A mining robot has an integrated drill arm, a cutting arm, and finer manipulators that allow it to sort through the rubble it creates. A typical model also has built-in harmonic resonators to soften earth and stone, making it easier for the robot to burrow into the ground. Construction and terraforming enterprises employ similar models of these industrial robots.

The dwarven mining corporation Ulrikka Clanholdings is known to make the best mining robots the galaxy has to offer. Outfitted with sturdy magma blades, these constructs can slice through rock like a heated knife cuts through butter. Ulrikka sells the robots to other mining outfits as a profitable side operation. The company sells at a premium, and tight contracts ensure a purchaser's intended usage doesn't conflict with Ulrikka interests. Occasionally, warriors and gladiators with a flair for the dramatic purchase a defunct mining robot and strip off the drill for use as an exotic and deadly weapon.

# TENEBROUS WORM

**CR 8**

**XP 4,800**

N Medium outsider (extraplanar)

**Init** +3; **Senses** darkvision 60 ft.; **Perception** +16

## DEFENSE
**HP** 125

**EAC** 20; **KAC** 22

**Fort** +12; **Ref** +10; **Will** +7

**Defensive Abilities** poisonous bristles; **Immunities** acid

## OFFENSE

**Speed** 20 ft.

**Melee** bite +17 (1d8+11 P plus shadow acid; critical corrode 1d6)

## STATISTICS

**Str** +3; **Dex** +3; **Con** +6; **Int** –4; **Wis** +0; **Cha** –2

**Skills** Stealth +16

## ECOLOGY

**Environment** any land (Shadow Plane)

**Organization** solitary, pair, swarm (3–6)

## SPECIAL ABILITIES

**Poisonous Bristles (Su)** Bristles of shadow extend from between the tenebrous worm's armored plates. Each time a creature within 10 feet of the worm attacks it, several of these bristles reactively shoot off at the attacker. The attacker must succeed at a DC 16 Reflex save or take 1d4 piercing damage and be exposed to tenebrous worm poison (see below). An attacker that strikes the worm with an unarmed strike or grapples the worm is automatically damaged and exposed to the poison.

**Shadow Acid (Su)** A tenebrous worm's bite delivers a mystical acid that dissolves organic matter into wisps of shadow. In dim light, this acid deals 3d6 acid damage. In normal light, it deals 2d6 acid damage. In bright light or darkness, it deals 1d6 acid damage.

## TENEBROUS WORM POISON

**Type** poison (injury); **Save** Fortitude DC 16

**Track** Dexterity (special);

    **Frequency** 1/round for 6 rounds

**Effect** progression track is Healthy–Sluggish–Stiffened–Staggered–Immobile; no end state.

**Cure** 2 consecutive saves

A tenebrous worm is the larval stage of the gloomwing (see page 56), but this young creature is more dangerous than the adult. When young hatch from the eggs a gloomwing lays in an unfortunate victim, the strongest among the hatchlings sometimes kills and eats its siblings. Other times, the larvae remain together in a pack or scatter into the surrounding environment to hunt.

Tenebrous worms crave flesh, and they eat it in whatever form they find, it's already carrion or living prey they've hunted down.

A tenebrous worm's belly is pale to the point of translucence, and its organs churn with shadowy fluids visible through its segmented carapace. As the worm grows, these liquids mix and partially solidify, poking out between the creature's plates to form poisonous bristles. A similar substance fills a reservoir near its mandibles, but this substance turns flesh to shadow that the worm consumes to supplement its diet of meat.

When a tenebrous worm has fed enough, it finds a hiding place where it can spin a cocoon of shadowy silk. This chrysalis absorbs surrounding light, reducing nonmagical bright and normal light to dim light in a radius of 20 feet. A tenebrous worm transforms inside the cocoon, emerging after several days as a gloomwing. The cocoon's remains, tattered gray sheets of silk, lose their light-absorbing properties.

# VELSTRAC, CANTOR

LE Small outsider (evil, extraplanar, lawful, velstrac)

**Init** +6; **Senses** darkvision 60 ft.; **Perception** +17

## DEFENSE      HP 120

**EAC** 21; **KAC** 22

**Fort** +8; **Ref** +10; **Will** +12

**Defensive Abilities** regeneration 5 (good or silver); **DR** 5/good or silver; **Immunities** cold

## OFFENSE

**Speed** 30 ft.

**Melee** claw +18 (2d6+9 S plus lingering touch)

**Offensive Abilities** unnerving gaze (30 ft., DC 18), waking nightmare

**Spell-Like Abilities** (CL 9th)

1/day–*nightmare* (DC 20), *shadow body* (see page 52)

3/day–*paranoia* (DC 19; see page 52)

At will–*lesser confusion* (DC 18)

## STATISTICS

**Str** +0; **Dex** +6; **Con** +2; **Int** +1; **Wis** +4; **Cha** +3

**Skills** Acrobatics +22, Bluff +17, Mysticism +17, Stealth +17

**Languages** Common, Infernal; telepathy 100 ft.

## ECOLOGY

**Environment** any (Shadow Plane)

**Organization** solitary, pair, expedition (3–6)

## SPECIAL ABILITIES

**Lingering Touch (Su)** A creature that takes damage from a velstrac cantor's claw must succeed at a DC 18 Will saving throw or the pain lingers in its mind, dealing 1d4 additional damage (2d4 if the cantor scored a critical hit) at the start of each of its turns for 1 minute. At the end of each of its turns, the target can attempt another saving throw to end this effect. Each of the cantor's additional successful attacks against a creature suffering this effect extends the duration by 1 round. Any form of magical healing ends this effect immediately. This is a mind-affecting effect.

**Unnerving Gaze (Su)** A cantor's appearance causes shock and sympathetic pain. A creature that fails its save against this mind-affecting fear effect is shaken for 1 round.

**Waking Nightmare (Su)** Once per minute as a full action, a cantor can mouth a soundless scream to create an illusory double of itself that is Large and even more horrifying. Creatures within 30 feet of and able to see the cantor must succeed at a DC 18 Will saving throw or believe this illusory double to be real. At the same moment, the cantor becomes invisible (as per *greater invisibility*). These effects last as long as at least one creature believes the illusion, but no longer than 1 minute. Both effects also end if the cantor is ever more than 30 feet away from the illusion at the end of its turn. The illusion appears to attack each round on the cantor's turn, and the cantor usually attacks the same target, gaining the benefits of both invisibility and stealth. After a creature attacks the illusion, the creature can attempt another save to disbelieve the effect. A creature exposed to this effect is immune to the same cantor's waking nightmare for 24 hours.

Only about 3 feet tall and weighing no more than 50 pounds, a cantor resembles a human child or halfling whose skin has been flayed, exposing the underlying musculature and connective tissue. Rather than being a bloody mess, however, its flesh is dull and gray. A cantor's glossy black eyes burn red when the creature becomes violent or uses its vile powers.

A cantor velstrac is a fiend that uses its horrific appearance as a weapon. It considers itself to be an instrument in an ongoing effort to help mortals accept the velstrac notion of reality–that pain is a tool of self-exploration and development. Cantors pursue this end through subterfuge and by aiding other velstracs as scouts.

# VOID OOZE

N Medium ooze

**Init** +2; **Senses** blindsight (vibration) 60 ft., sightless;
   **Perception** +14

**Aura** shadow siphon (20 ft.)

## DEFENSE
**HP** 105

**EAC** 19; **KAC** 21

**Fort** +11; **Ref** +7; **Will** +4

**Defensive Abilities** void adaptation; **Immunities** ooze
   immunities; **Resistances** cold 5

## OFFENSE

**Speed** 20 ft., climb 20 ft.

**Melee** pseudopod +17 (1d6+11 B plus 1d6 cold and
   numb senses)

## STATISTICS

**Str** +4; **Dex** +2; **Con** +5; **Int** —; **Wis** +0; **Cha** –3

**Skills** Stealth +19

**Other Abilities** mindless, split

## ECOLOGY

**Environment** any (Shadow Plane)

**Organization** solitary, pair, or gloom (3–6)

## SPECIAL ABILITIES

**Numb Senses (Su)** When a void ooze
hits with a pseudopod attack, the
target must succeed at a DC 15
Fortitude saving throw or its senses
are shrouded for 1 round as if the
creature were in a dark void. The
target is blinded and deafened,
as well as unable to smell,
taste, and feel subtle sensations. A
target's blindsense and blindsight are also
ineffective for the duration.

**Shadow Siphon (Su)** Nonmagical bright or normal
light within 20 feet of a void ooze is reduced to
dim light. If a dying creature in this aura
loses a Resolve Point or spends any
Resolve Points to stabilize, the
ooze regains 10 Hit Points. If a
creature dies in the aura, the
ooze regains 10 Hit Points.
If the ooze enters the space
of a dead creature, the
creature's body disintegrates
into fine black ash and the
ooze regains 10 Hit Points.

**Split (Ex)** If a void ooze would
regain more Hit Points from
its shadow siphon ability than its
Hit Point maximum, it instead splits into
two identical oozes, each with Hit Points equal
to half the original's current total plus half the Hit

Points the original ooze would have regained.

Void oozes originate from the lightless depths of outer space on the Shadow Plane. They are drawn to open interplanar portals and to areas where the barriers between dimensions are weak. Life, especially when coupled with warmth, attracts these creatures like the stench of death attracts carrion birds. The oozes feed on the subtle negative energy surrounding the dying and recently dead, using that energy to reproduce.

These creatures can hibernate indefinitely, and they are inured to outer space and airless environments. Because of these traits, void oozes can be found almost anywhere. Explorers have encountered them on planets (habitable or not), asteroids, and spacedocks. The oozes have also been found aboard vessels that have traveled in the darkest regions of space, where the oozes attached themselves to the hull of a passing starship.

# KAX

*Lonely Planet in a Starless Void*

**Diameter:** ×1; **Mass:** ×1
**Gravity:** Standard
**Location:** The Vast
**Atmosphere:** Normal
**Day:** 48 hours; **Year:** 2 years

Kax is a lush world with diverse biomes. Rather than being composed of large continents, it is covered in thousands of extensive archipelagos, several of which surround enormous islands. It has a broad tropical zone at its equator and ice caps at each pole, but most of the planet is temperate enough that settlements can be established anywhere without requiring much in the way of advanced shelters. Native flora and fauna tend to be huge and carnivorous, including dinosaurs and pack predators, which are most active at night. The fruit and vegetables that naturally grow across the planet are consumable by most Pact Worlds species, and many find them sweet smelling and delicious.

Kax is also the only planet in its system, and from the planet's surface and surrounding space, no stars other than its own sun are visible. There are no moons, no asteroids, and no other objects of any kind floating nearby. As a result, no one knows where Kax actually is.

This "lonely planet" (as it is sometimes called) can be reached only by Drift travel, and the navigational beacons used to locate it place it in the Vast, but its exact location in the galaxy (if it is even in this galaxy) remains a mystery. The inability to see any stars from the Kax system is generally assumed to be the result of a nebula or dust cloud that cuts off their distant light, but if so, the concealment is total. No evidence, scientific or magical, has yet explained this occlusion.

After Kax was discovered, decades after the advent of Drift travel, it was briefly a common destination for research vessels and colony ships hoping to settle on the vibrant world. However, early expeditions suffered catastrophic losses. Ships sent distress calls that warned of infection, mutiny, or both, and later expeditions found them with all hands dead. Settlements reported an increase in minor accidents and theft, then stopped reporting in entirely. Some were found abandoned, while others were never found at all. Most famously, the Golden Vault colony funded by AbadarCorp was discovered entirely deserted by a supply ship's crew—colonists' possessions still in lockers, food rotting in larders—with no sign or record of what happened to the nearly 2,000 residents.

Theories to explain what happens on Kax run wild. Many believe the planet is used as a base of operation by some violent organization, with suggestions ranging from the Corpse Fleet to grays and reptoids. More extraordinary theories include the idea that the entire world (and its star) are haunted by the spirits of long-dead aliens, that the system is actually a demiplane that periodically fades away and ejects all non-native sentient beings into space, or that it is connected to the First World by several "thin spots" where angry fey emerge to kidnap any who dare despoil the planet. Attempts to confirm or debunk these theories find nothing, and some research expeditions have disappeared entirely. As a result, travel to Kax has greatly reduced in recent years.

## THE PENUMBRA PROTOCOL

*by Jenny Jarzabski*

Infected with a sickness that threatens to turn them into twisted sadists, the heroes travel to the city of Cuvacara on the planet Verces to find the possible origin of their affliction! They soon discover that a sinister company plans to release a new social media app that will corrupt the entire city. If they can survive attacks from corporate assassins, the heroes must shut down the transmitters set to broadcast the corrupting signal in order to save the metropolis. Along the way, they learn the location of the company's hidden underground base on the planet's Darkside, where a sinister executive awaits their arrival.

## CUVACARA

*by Jenny Jarzabski*

A bustling metropolis bathed in eternal twilight, Cuvacara is the capital city of the nation of Vimal in the terminator zone of the tidally locked planet of Verces. Learn about the diverse residents of the Dusk Jewel, the multitude of corporations that have their offices there, and the notorious transactions that occur in the city's darkened alleys. In addition, discover a handful of new Vercite cybernetic augmentations.

## FIENDS OF SHADOW

*By Isabelle Lee*

Self-stylized artists whose medium is flesh and bone, the outsiders known as velstracs are devious and amoral fiends. From their dark lairs on the Shadow Plane, they seek to bring their twisted form of enlightenment to mortals. Explore a menu of magitech modifications created by velstracs that only the daring and foolhardy use for themselves.

## SUBSCRIBE TO STARFINDER ADVENTURE PATH

The Signal of Screams Adventure Path continues! Don't miss out on a single exciting volume—head over to **paizo.com/starfinder** and subscribe today to have Starfinder Roleplaying Game, Starfinder Adventure Path, and Starfinder Accessories products delivered to your door!